IN THE STUDIO

PAINTING THE FIGURE
IN WATERCOLOR

Herb Olsen, A.N.A.

 VAN NOSTRAND REINHOLD COMPANY
NEW YORK   CINCINNATI   TORONTO   LONDON   MELBOURNE

CONTENTS

COLOR PLATES

To my wife, Doris

FOREWORD

In the beginning God created man in His own image and the world has never ceased to marvel at the perfection of His creation. Though man has failed morally, the physical beauty of the body has inspired painters and sculptors throughout the ages and continues to challenge the artist of today.

Countless books of instruction have been written to guide the oil painter, but to my knowledge very little has been written about painting the figure in watercolor. The increasing popularity of watercolor has brought about the need for an instructive, simplified explanation of how the figure is painted in this medium.

Figure painting is not for the complete beginner, but the step-by-step explanations in this book should be of help to the not-too-experienced artist. He will find the sections on basic forms and the six-step figure of special interest.

In describing painting procedures, I have repeatedly used the phrase: "After a careful drawing has been completed." Figure painting requires a good working knowledge of drawing and anatomy, but in a book concerned primarily with painting it would be impossible to cover these subjects thoroughly. The section on "Drawing the Figure"—which contains suggestions on simplified procedures of particular value to those who have not tried figure studies before—is intended primarily to stimulate an interest that will lead to further, more intensive study of anatomy.

Any type of figure may be a thing of beauty when seen with the special vision of an artist. Lean, fat, short, tall, young, old, light, dark, male or female—all are fit subjects for paintings. Of course, each artist has his own preferences. My vote, as the illustrations throughout this book will show, is for the lithe, graceful feminine figure.

Figure painting is often thought of as being limited to the painting of nudes and semidraped figures. This is not true. Small-scale figures and groups of figures can add much interest to a landscape or street scene and there are many examples of this in these pages. However, even these small figures require some basic knowledge of figure painting.

Because backgrounds are important—even in figure painting—I have shown a variety of indoor and outdoor settings and in many cases have included step-by-step descriptions of how they were painted.

It is my sincere hope that my approach to painting the figure—which is by no means the only one, nor necessarily the best—may be of help to other painters interested in the fascinating medium of watercolor.

The thoughts which these few pages clothe with words
Will not convince some minds that all they read
Is truth. But if the reading shall provoke
Some wiser student to dispute the facts
Assumed and find conclusions which will solve
One honest doubt, we have not wrought in vain.

FROM "BEGINNINGS"

BY JAMES BATTERSON

MATERIALS

While good materials of themselves will never guarantee a good picture, no artist can do his best without them. Paper, colors and brushes of good quality are much easier to work with than inferior materials and more likely therefore to produce better—and more permanent—paintings.

paper

The choice of paper depends on the artist's personal preferences, on the way he works, the effects he wants to achieve. The rough, irregular surface of a heavy, hand-made paper is preferred by many because it takes to watercolor so well. It doesn't buckle or wrinkle under heavy washes, it can be scrubbed and scraped without serious injury, and the irregularity of its surface texture often contributes interesting accidental effects to the painting.

All the paintings reproduced in color in this book were painted on rough, heavy handmade papers—either 300 lb. D'Arches or 400 lb. A.W.S. (American Watercolor Society).

For some types of work, however, a smoother surface is desirable. Watercolors intended for reproduction as magazine illustrations are often done on smooth-textured papers or illustration boards. Most of the paintings reproduced in black and white in this book were done on cold-pressed Stuart Board.

In watercolor painting a poor grade of paper is never an economy. It will buckle, wrinkle, turn color—and its stamped-pattern surface will be difficult to work on and distracting to look at, especially in a figure painting.

However, if you must economize, you might want to try using a lighter weight paper mounted on a stretcher to make it tight and strong. Some artists prefer to work this way. For this purpose a 140 lb. paper is a good weight. First wet the paper thoroughly, perhaps by soaking it in the bathtub. Then, while it is wet, tack it firmly to a stretcher frame being sure to pull it taut. Let it dry completely before starting to paint. You can use a Rothbro paper stretcher or you can make your own.

brushes

Good quality sable brushes in several sizes are essential equipment for all watercolor painting. For the paintings in this book I used sables #2, #5, #8 and #12, Grumbacher's flat Aquarelle, and the fan brush shown on page 16. I also used several short-hair flat bristle brushes—#2, #7 and #12.

Proper care of good brushes is important and will pay off in longer wear and more dependable results. After every painting session, be sure to clean your brushes with soap and water and wipe them with a rag before putting them away.

colors

Top quality colors are made by several leading manufacturers. The brand used is a matter of personal choice. But don't be tempted by the seeming economy of cheaper grades. Even for a beginner, student colors spell wasted time and effort. Probably nothing is more frustrating when laying in a wash than to reach for color and then have to work so hard and so long trying to get it off the palette that the wash dries before you get the color you're after. The time con-

Maskoid was applied to all areas that were to remain white. After the background and dress areas were painted, the Maskoid was removed with a rubber cement pick-up.

After the painting was completed, I used a mat knife to scratch and gouge out certain areas to indicate foam and spray.

The white areas in the girl's dress are the areas of white paper that were protected by the Maskoid.

The white lines and dots scratched out with the mat knife make the painting sparkle.

sumed in trying to gouge color off a palette with inferior paints is in itself a good reason for using good paints. But further than that, no matter how much time or effort is put into it, the depth of color simply will not be there in the cheaper grades.

As long as you use reputable, high-grade colors, you will not have to worry about the permanency of the pigments—with the possible exception of alizarin crimson which may have a tendency to fade and should be used sparingly.

accessories

In addition to his basic equipment—paper, brushes and colors—the watercolor painter needs certain accessories. Every artist has a tendency to develop his own list of special tools. Those mentioned below are ones I have found to be especially useful.

Maskoid is a liquid masking solution which forms a waterproof film when dry. It is used to preserve areas of the paper that are to remain white. It should be applied very carefully with a brush—but this is one time a good brush should not be used. It can be peeled off later (using a rubber cement pick-up or a piece of dried Maskoid) without damaging the paper or affecting the surrounding areas already painted. The usefulness of Maskoid is demonstrated in several of the step-by-step painting procedures throughout the book, particularly on pages 48-49 and 138-139. A word of caution about Maskoid: Don't use it in the hot sun; it becomes gummy in the heat and is impossible to remove.

A small natural silk cosmetic sponge (not rubber) can be very useful when you want to delete areas already painted. On page 132 you can see how I sponged out an area of a completed painting in order to add a figure. The final result is in color on page 134.

Rags have many uses of course. One you

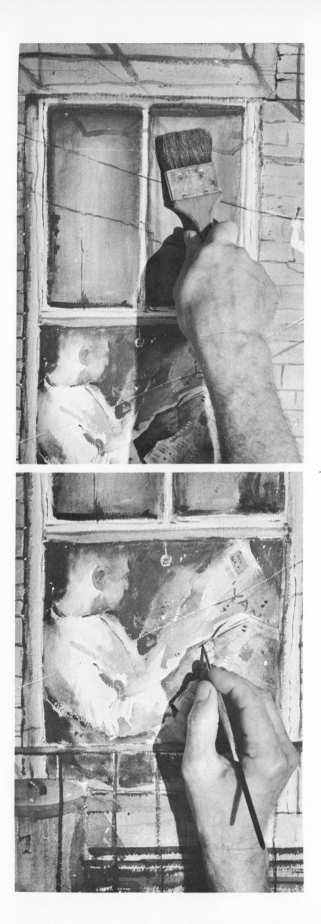

Color was applied to the window panes using a single stroke of a two-inch brush. A wipe of a rag gave the effect of light reflections on the panes.

For tiny details such as accents on the hands and the newspaper, a #2 brush was used. If this small brush were used for larger areas, however, the painting would have a scubby look.

While the sky area was still wet, it was stroked and patted with a crumbled clean cotton rag. This broke up the blue area of the sky and created cloud effects. Darker blue tones were then inserted.

might not think of is to create cloud effects. Sky area is painted and then, while still damp, wiped with a cotton rag. A sponge can also be used this way.

A mat knife is helpful in producing sparkle in a painting. Use a knife with a heavy cast-iron handle; it is easier to control than a light-weight knife. It is used to achieve special effects, such as rain flecks (as seen in the painting on page 139, "Figures in Fog"), weeds, highlights on stone (see "Ripples in the Sand" on page 83), water (see "Waterfall" on page 117) and numerous other effects (see "Harbor at Strawberry Bank" on pages 156-157, "Baltimore Street Scene" on page 143, and "Zoo" on pages 122-123).

Sandpaper is useful in achieving certain special effects in landscape. See "Columbus Circle" on page 137 and "Sailboats" on page 161.

A sand eraser can also be used for textural effects, but it is even more useful in correcting mistakes since it can bring back the white of the paper in limited areas.

A kneaded eraser is essential for erasing pencil lines because it doesn't leave crumbs, which can be bothersome while applying a wash.

A mirror is an especially useful accessory. It is the painter's third eye and fresh viewpoint. For some reason, the mirror-reversed image of the painting emphasizes mistakes in color, values and composition that might otherwise go unnoticed, and by doubling the distance between the artist and the painting, it enables the artist to see whether his painting holds together.

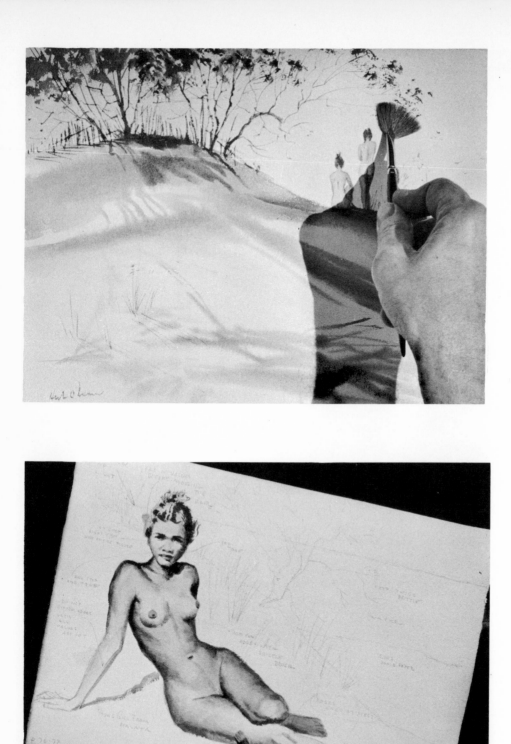

In using the fan brush for effects such as the casual-looking splotches of leaves in "At the Dunes," the paint is patted on rather than stroked. After the sky wash had dried, using the fan brush I painted the lighter leaves with Hooker's green, yellow ochre and orange. When this was dry, the darker leaves were added—again using the fan brush—with sepia, orange, and Hooker's green. The fan brush can also be used for weeds, grass, and shrubbery.

The short-hair bristle brush is an excellent tool for softening hard edges. It can be used even after the paper has dried. The only requisite is a rough, heavy (at least 300 lb.) paper. Anything lighter will buckle and the brush will streak the edges of a smooth paper.

The brush is held much as a pen is held in writing and a wrist action is used. Care should be taken not to get too much water on the brush and of course no color should be used—just clean water. Working with half-closed eyes makes it easier to see the edges meld.

Further suggestions for using the bristle brush will be found on the painting "Girl from Malaya" on pages 46-47.

REFLECTIONS IN THE WATER

There are many special techniques in watercolor painting that can be used to suggest textures. Some of them have been mentioned on the previous pages. In painting "Reflections in the Water" I used two more.

To get the sandy effect in the streaky section at the upper left, for instance, I used the heel of the brush, rather dry, dragging it in short horizontal strokes. To indicate the pebbles scattered around the beach, I dipped a damp, coarse, irregular sponge into the colors on the palette and then, using a straight arm movement, let the sponge kiss the paper.

The enlarged detail, which is reproduced at the exact size of the original, shows these strokes and textures very distinctly. Seen from normal viewing range, of course, they blend together to create the effects seen in the reproduction of the painting as a whole.

REFLECTIONS IN THE WATER

FULL SIZE DETAIL

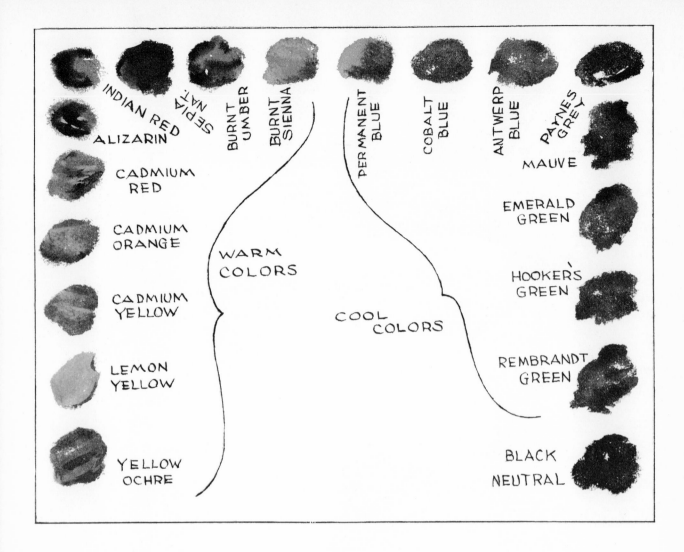

INDIAN RED
SEPIA NAT.
BURNT UMBER
BURNT SIENNA
ALIZARIN
CADMIUM RED
CADMIUM ORANGE
CADMIUM YELLOW
LEMON YELLOW
YELLOW OCHRE

WARM COLORS

COOL COLORS

PERMANENT BLUE
COBALT BLUE
ANTWERP BLUE
PAYNES GREY
MAUVE
EMERALD GREEN
HOOKER'S GREEN
REMBRANDT GREEN
BLACK NEUTRAL

THE PALETTE

A palette for figure painting is the same as a palette for landscapes, as you will see if you compare the palette above with the one used in "Watercolor Made Easy" (Reinhold, 1956).

I use a large (19 inches by 13 inches) butcher's tray which can hold a wide assortment of pigments in generous amounts with ample room left for mixing colors. It's wise to keep plenty of pigment on your palette so you won't run out of color in the middle of a wash. Don't worry about the pigments hardening—good quality colors can be left for long periods of time. If they do show signs of cracking after a while, a drop or two of glycerine will soften them.

The colors on my palette are arranged in groups from warm to cool. This plan works very well for me, but it is not the only arrangement possible and perhaps not the best one for you. It is most helpful, however, to have a definite plan for your palette so you can reach for the right color almost unconsciously—as automatically as a typist reaches for the right key or a pianist for the right note.

21

DRAWING THE FIGURE

Before you can become a figure painter, you must first learn to draw the figure; and to draw the figure correctly, you must know a good deal about the complex structure that is the human body—how the bones and muscles are put together, what they can do and, perhaps most important, what they cannot do.

Anatomy is a subject that requires far more space than it is possible to give it in a book concerned primarily with painting techniques, but in the following pages you will find some suggestions that should help you get started if you have had little or no experience drawing the figure. If you are ready for more detailed information, you will find there are many books that deal with anatomy alone.

Figure drawings range from quick, rough sketches of fleeting action and detailed studies of construction to finished drawings made for their own sake. The drawing opposite was done with lithographic pencil and wash after several preliminary sketches established the composition. "Girl with Telephone" is a pen-and-ink drawing on scratchboard, the scratchboard tool having been used to lighten heavy pen strokes.

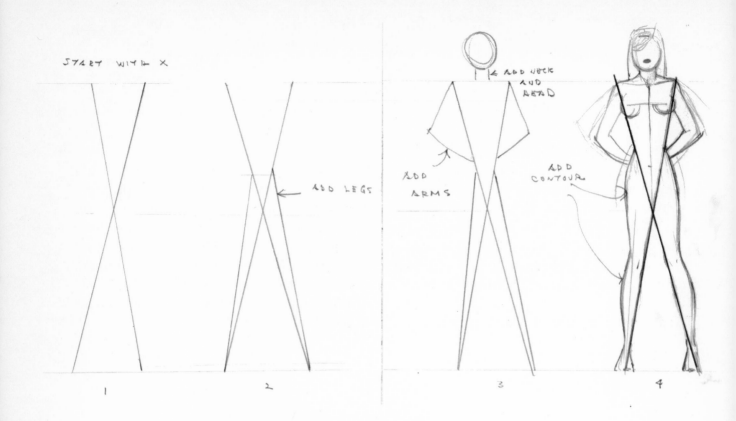

START WITH X

ADD LEGS

ADD NECK AND HEAD

ADD ARMS

ADD CONTOUR

1   2   3   4

BASIC FORMS

Simple familiar forms—triangles, pear shapes, forms like the letter "Y" or the letter "X"—can serve as a framework for figure drawings and often will even suggest the pose of the model in reasonably accurate proportion.

Examples of how such forms can be adapted to poses of figures standing, sitting, reclining, seen front view, back view or side view, are shown on pages 24 through 29.

Further on in the book, pages 42-43, a step-by-step demonstration shows the development of a figure from basic form to completed painting.

Practice in the imaginative use of basic forms can be especially helpful to the beginner as an introduction to figure drawing. Later, when he draws from the model, this ability to think in terms of shapes will be of tremendous value.

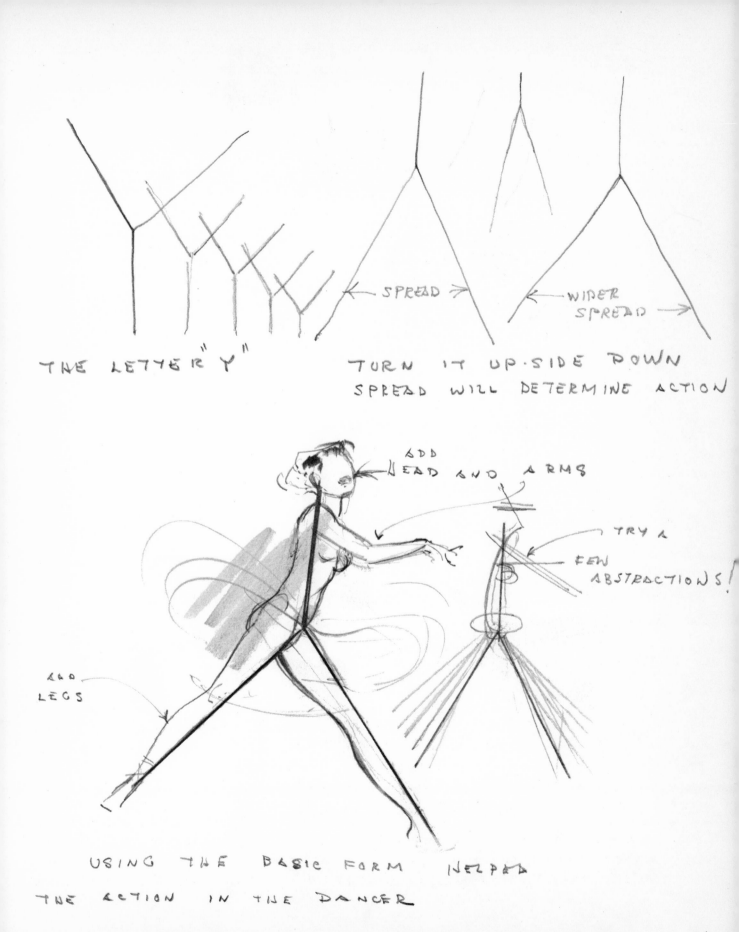

THE LETTER "Y"

TURN IT UP-SIDE DOWN
SPREAD WILL DETERMINE ACTION

SPREAD

WIDER SPREAD

ADD HEAD AND ARMS

TRY A FEW ABSTRACTIONS!

ADD LEGS

USING THE BASIC FORM HELPED
THE ACTION IN THE DANCER

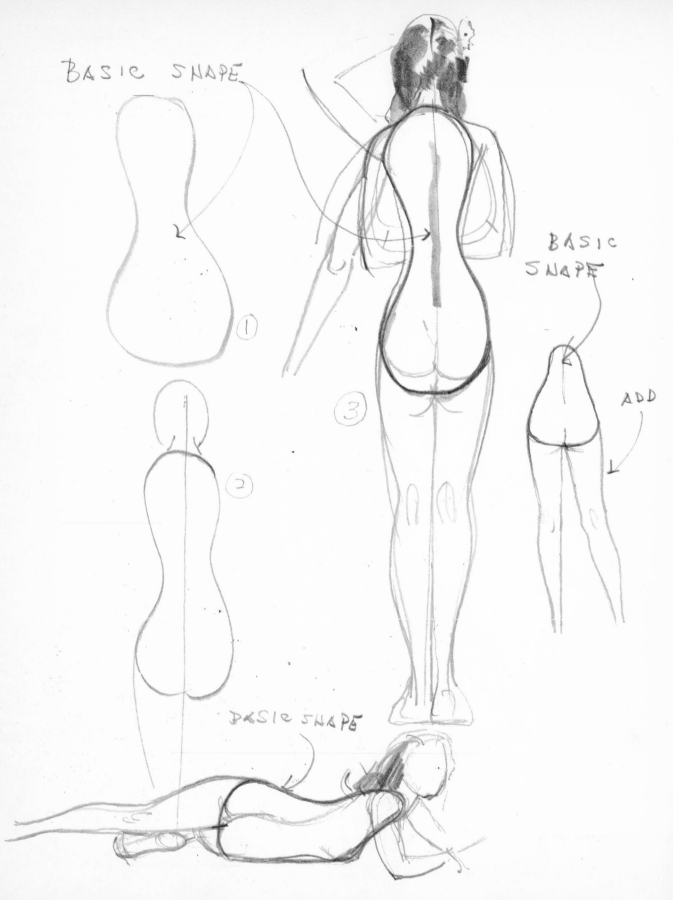

BASIC SHAPE

1

2

BASIC SHAPE

ADD

3

BASIC SHAPE

26

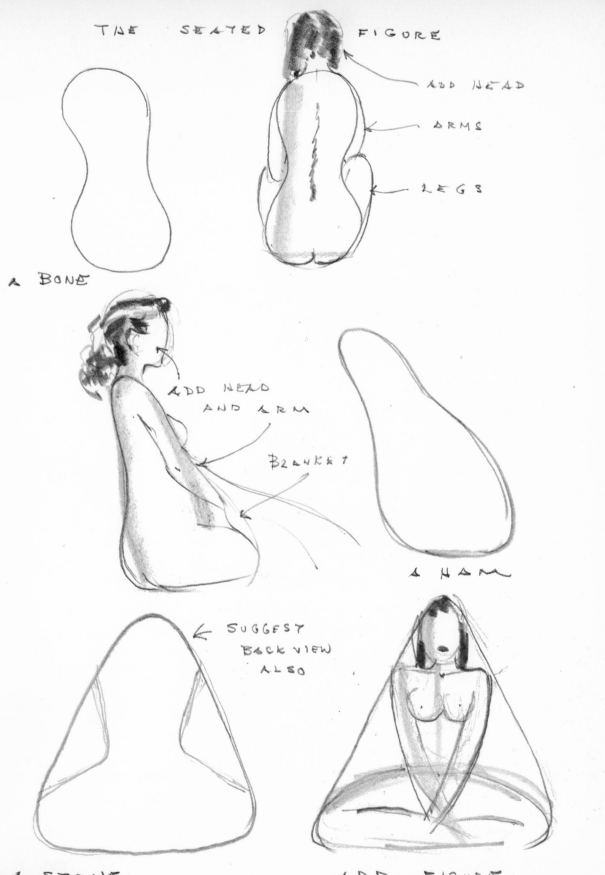

THE SEATED FIGURE

ADD HEAD

ARMS

LEGS

A BONE

ADD HEAD
AND ARM

BLANKET

A HAM

SUGGEST
BACK VIEW
ALSO

A STONE

ADD FIGURE

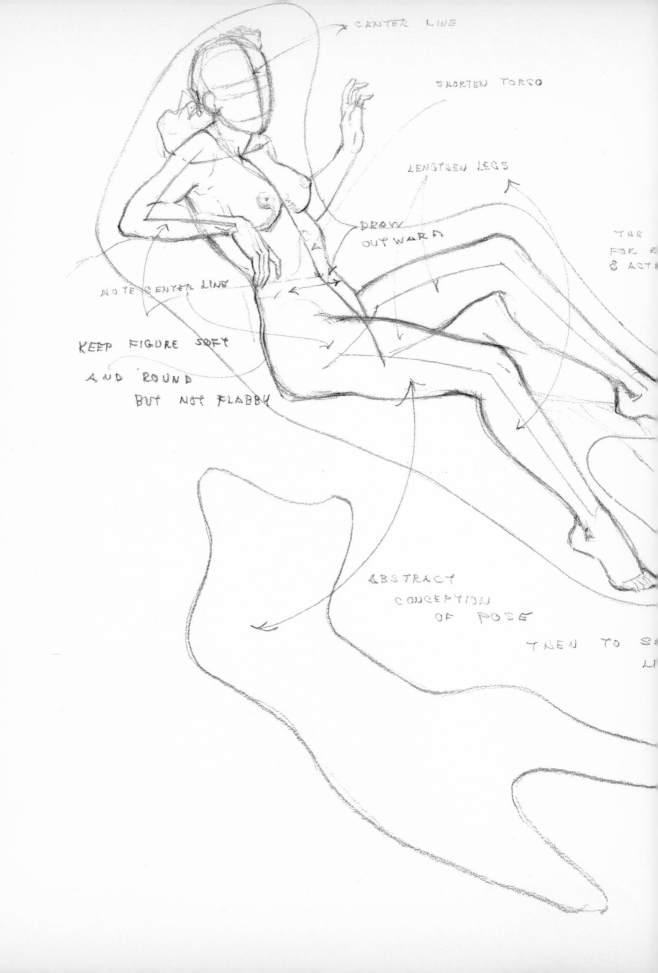

CENTER LINE

SHORTEN TORSO

LENGTHEN LEGS

THE
FOR
& ACT

DRAW
OUTWARD

NOTE CENTER LINE

KEEP FIGURE SOFT
AND ROUND
BUT NOT FLABBY

ABSTRACT
CONCEPTION
OF POSE

THEN TO S
LI

28

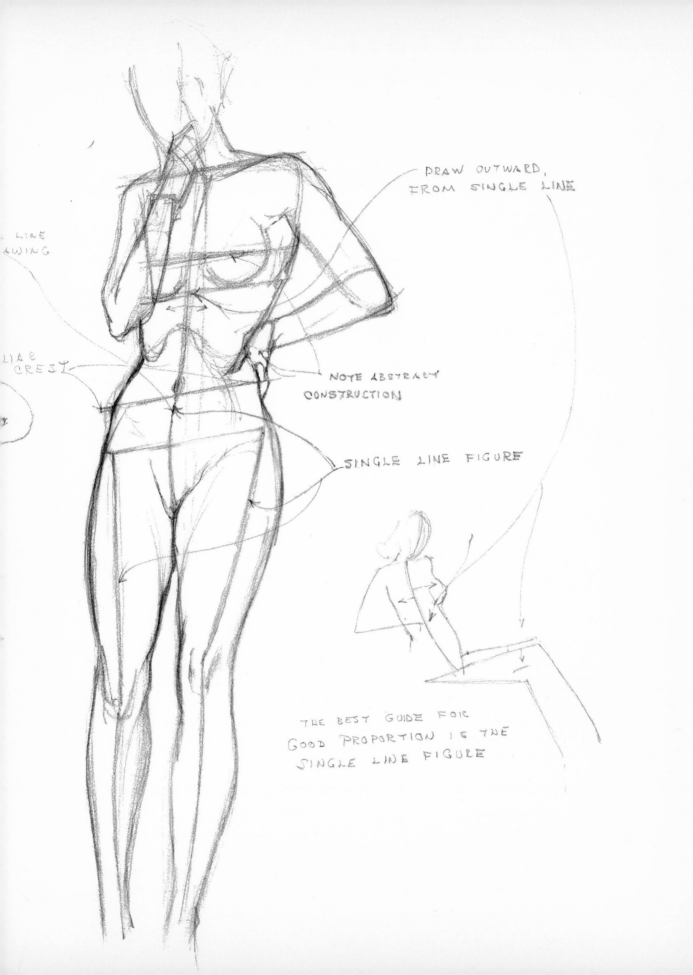

DRAW OUTWARD,
FROM SINGLE LINE

LINE
DRAWING

ILIAC
CREST

NOTE ABSTRACT
CONSTRUCTION

SINGLE LINE FIGURE

THE BEST GUIDE FOR
GOOD PROPORTION IS THE
SINGLE LINE FIGURE

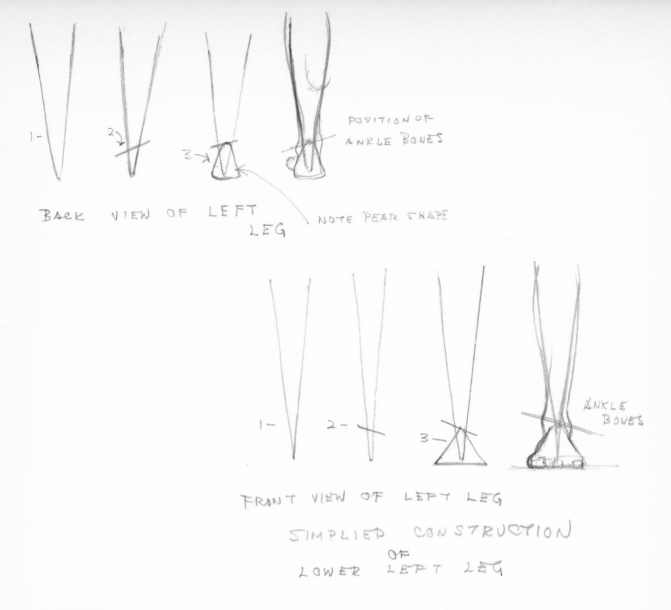

BACK VIEW OF LEFT LEG

POSITION OF ANKLE BONES

NOTE PEAR SHAPE

FRONT VIEW OF LEFT LEG

ANKLE BONES

SIMPLIED CONSTRUCTION
OF
LOWER LEFT LEG

PARTS

In painting the figure, it is not necessary to indicate all the muscles in every part of the body. However, it is necessary to understand the construction of each part in order to know how it functions and what its limitations are—how a leg or arm can bend, how far a head can turn.

On this and the following pages I have illustrated some of the major parts of the body without showing an overabundance of detail. On page 31 I've drawn the simplified muscular structures of the leg and arm—

with only the major muscles shown. The further simplification of the leg on page 32 was made possible by the knowledge of its construction indicated on page 31.

Simplification of the muscular structure is important, especially in drawing the female figure, where muscles are less apparent than in the male. Too much muscle detail is unattractive and unnecessary—unless it is being done for study purposes.

To achieve proficiency in drawing the figure, practice drawing each part separately.

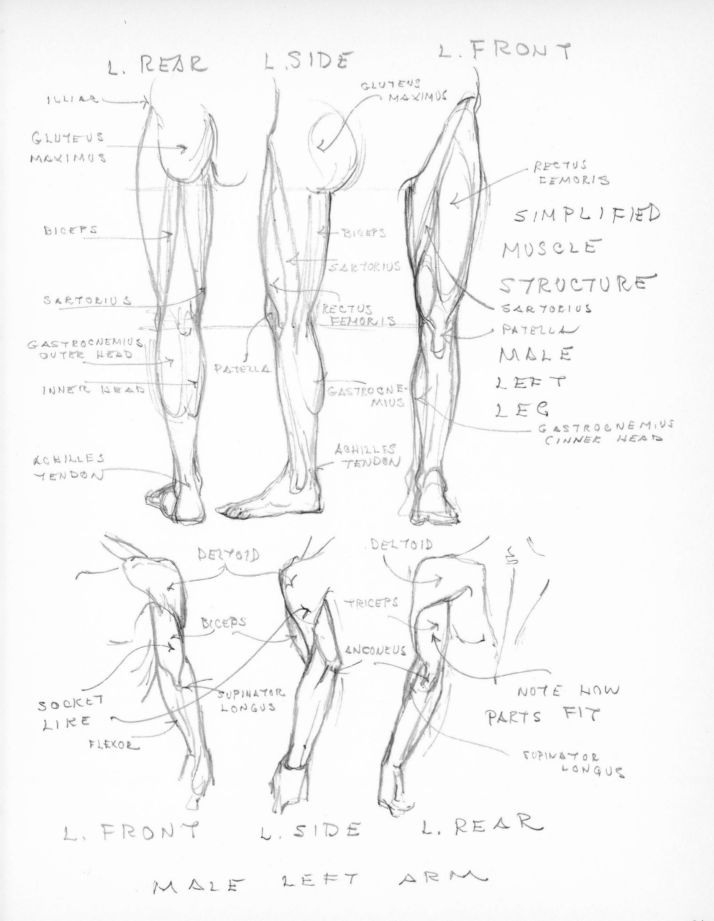

L. REAR   L. SIDE   L. FRONT

ILLIAC

GLUTEUS
MAXIMUS

GLUTEUS
MAXIMUS

BICEPS

SARTORIUS

GASTROCNEMIUS
OUTER HEAD

INNER HEAD

ACHILLES
TENDON

BICEPS

SARTORIUS

RECTUS
FEMORIS

PATELLA

GASTROCNE-
MIUS

ACHILLES
TENDON

RECTUS
FEMORIS

SIMPLIFIED
MUSCLE
STRUCTURE

SARTORIUS

PATELLA

MALE
LEFT
LEG

GASTROCNEMIUS
(INNER HEAD

DELTOID   DELTOID

BICEPS

TRICEPS

ANCONEUS

SOCKET
LIKE

FLEXOR

SUPINATOR
LONGUS

NOTE HOW
PARTS FIT

SUPINATOR
LONGUS

L. FRONT   L. SIDE   L. REAR

MALE LEFT ARM

31

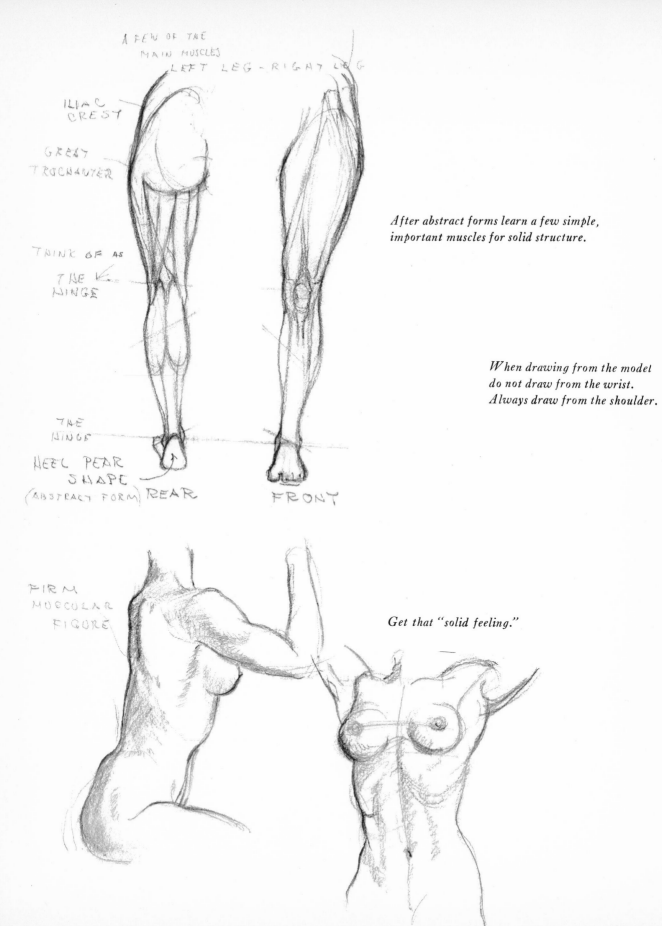

A FEW OF THE
MAIN MUSCLES
LEFT LEG - RIGHT LEG

ILIAC
CREST

GREAT
TROCHANTER

THINK OF AS
THE
HINGE

THE
HINGE

HEEL PEAR
SHAPE
(ABSTRACT FORM) REAR

FRONT

FIRM
MUSCULAR
FIGURE

*After abstract forms learn a few simple,
important muscles for solid structure.*

*When drawing from the model
do not draw from the wrist.
Always draw from the shoulder.*

Get that "solid feeling."

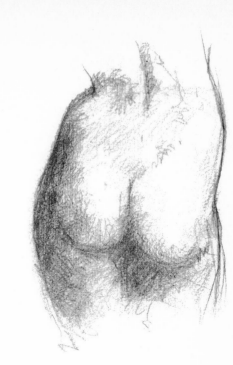

The pelvic area of the body gives the figure strong action. Learn this area thoroughly.

Concentrate on one part and learn it.

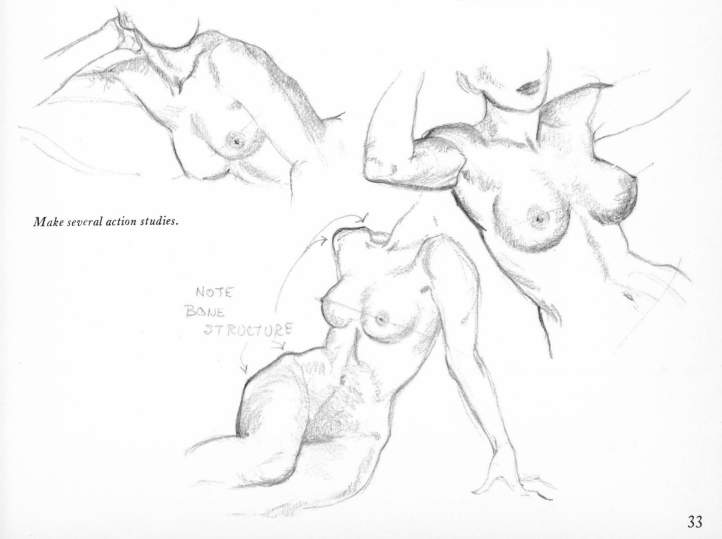

Make several action studies.

NOTE
BONE
STRUCTURE

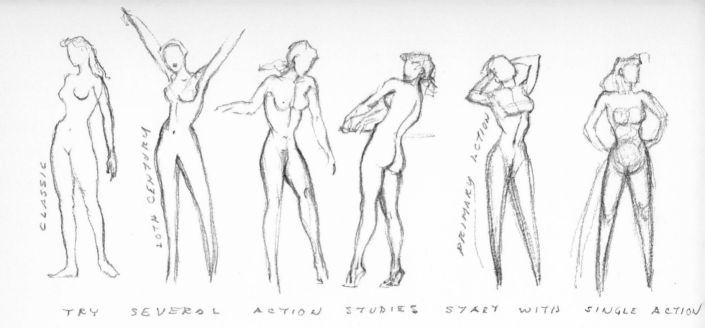

CLASSIC   20TH CENTURY   PRIMARY ACTION

TRY SEVERAL ACTION STUDIES START WITH SINGLE ACTION

ACTION SKETCHES

There is no better way to develop your ability to draw the figure than to practice making action sketches. You need basic knowledge of anatomical construction to begin with, but—like the musician at his scales—you will find that continued practice develops facility.

For action sketches, try to find a model who poses easily and gracefully—but don't copy the model slavishly. If you study anatomical drawings and learn something of how the bone and muscular structure of the body govern its movements, you will be able to draw what you know, not just what you see.

In making action sketches as an exercise, remember that action is not necessarily violent or even vigorous. A turn of the head or flick of the wrist may be subject enough for an action study—each requires knowledge of how connecting parts of the body move in relation to each other.

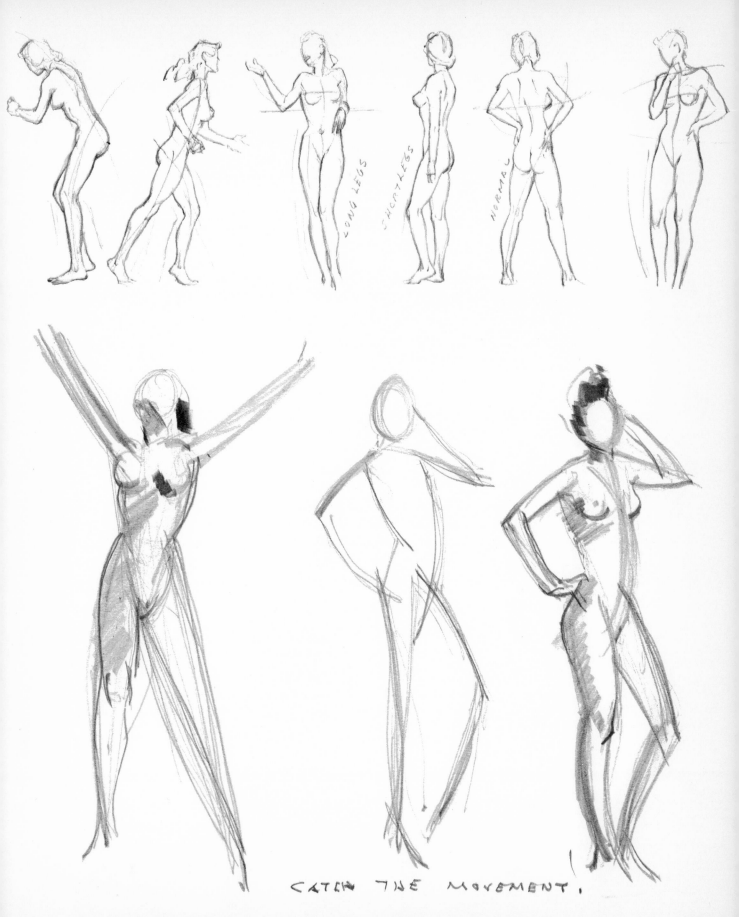

CATCH THE MOVEMENT.

35

WHEN MAKING
ACTION STUDIES BE
SURE TO DRAW
FROM YOUR ARM
NOT
YOUR WRIST

KEEP ACTION
FLOWING
EASILY

A FEW
ACTION
STUDIES

YOUNG
NEGRESS

USE A VARIED LINE

do not dig too deep at start

PAINT OUT YOUR MISTAKES

scratch Board

ACTION SKETCHES ON SCRATCHBOARD

The action sketches shown here were done on scratchboard, a special cardboard with a smooth white surface of hard chalk which lends itself to a very effective white-on-black drawing technique.

To make these drawings, the white scratchboard surface was first coated with ink. When this had dried thoroughly, a sharp pointed tool was used to make the drawings. It cut through the dark coating to reveal the white surface beneath and the drawings appear as white lines on a black background. It is possible, of course, to remove large areas of the ink and produce a black-on-white effect—but this technique is not well suited to action sketches.

In doing scratchboard drawings, only the coating should be scratched, never the board beneath. Mistakes can be corrected by repainting the area—the ink serving as eraser —but if the previous cuts have been too deep, the tool will tend to slip into the old grooves.

EXAGGERATED ACTION

To capture the peak moment in a vigorous action such as this one is difficult. No model can possibly hold it for more than a fraction of a second. Even a photograph, unless it's taken by an expert at stop-action photography, will be less than satisfactory. Here again you have to draw on what you know of anatomy to supplement what you actually see.

I used the photograph on this page as a basis for the painting opposite but notice how I exaggerated the action for a more dramatic effect. The model was not a dancer and the photograph was far from perfect, but that was just as well—there was no temptation to copy it directly.

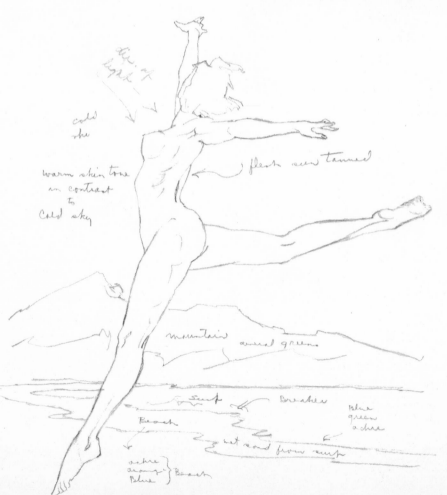

FROM BASIC SHAPE TO FINISHED PAINTING

This step-by-step series shows how the basic shape—discussed on pages 24-29—can be used as the framework for a figure painting. First, of course, sketches are made to establish a pose. Once this is decided on, the procedure is as follows:

step 1. *Make basic shape of the action.*

step 2. *Make single line drawing to indicate positions of arms, legs and torso to determine correct proportions.*

step 3. *Make careful drawing of figure over single-line framework.*

step 4. *Add chair and erase single-line framework. Apply wash of clear water over*

the figure to remove any oily film on the paper.

step 5. *When paper is dry, apply light wash of sepia to figure. This is tone 1. Leave towel and chair white.*

step 6. *When tone 1 is dry, apply tone 2 as indicated and let dry.*

step 7. *Add wash of tone 3 and let dry.*

step 8. *Finish by adding darkest notes (tone 4) for hair and dark accents. Soften hard edges with a bristle brush. If tonal values seem unrelated, add washes until lights and darks meld satisfactorily. Note that it is easier to see values with half-closed eyes.*

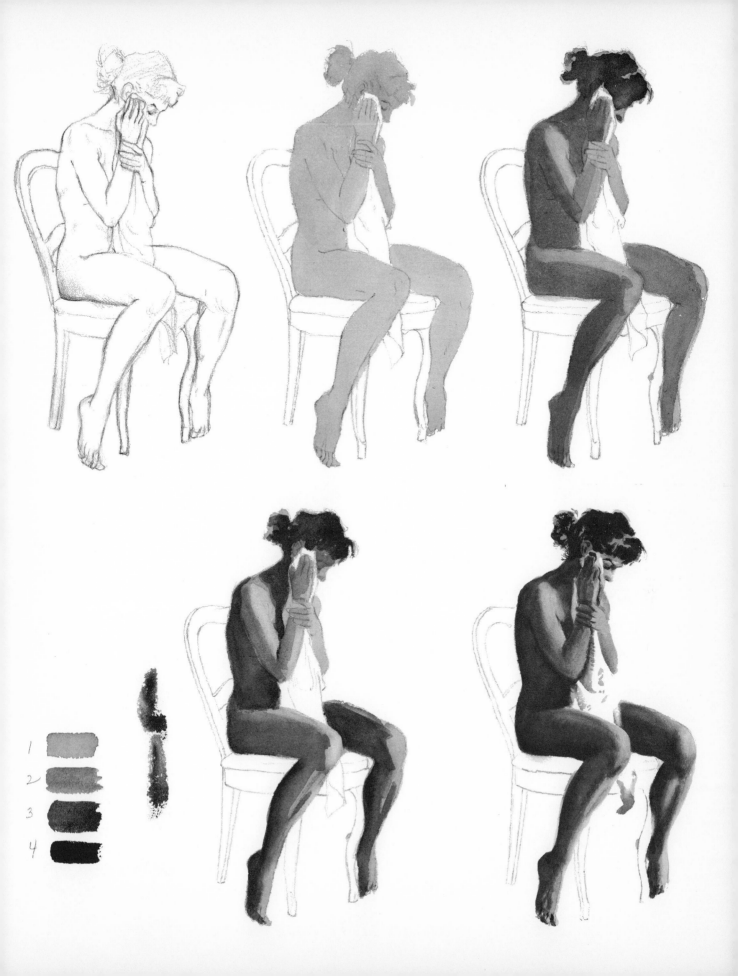

MONOCHROME TECHNIQUE

Although the nude has not traditionally been a favorite subject of the watercolor painter, one form of watercolor—the wash drawing—has long been a favorite of the figure painter. Monochrome watercolor is an excellent medium for figure sketches and studies as it quickly suggests both the fluid line and the solid form of the subject.

It has another, more important, advantage. Working with just one color—whether in quick, sketchy wash drawings or carefully painted monochrome watercolors—forces the artist to distinguish tonal values as

sharply as he might otherwise distinguish colors. Painting a figure in one color requires an eye for the subtle variations in tone that will show the modeling of the form. Once you have learned to see these tonal values and to paint them in washes of one color, you will find your ability to handle tonal values in full color has also improved.

The demonstration on pages 42-43 showed how just four tonal values of sepia were used to paint a figure. The painting opposite and those on the next few pages were painted in much the same way.

Here is another demonstration series showing how the figure can be modeled in four tones of one color.

A light wash of sepia was applied first (any one color could have been used). While the sepia wash was still wet, middle tones were added as accents. Modeling was completed while the washes were still wet. While the figure was still damp—but no longer wet—darks were added as indicated. If the wash had dried before modeling was satisfactory, the areas affected could have been slightly dampened and carefully repainted.

"Young Girl from Malaya" shows how the hard edges where washes of different tonal values meet can be softened by using a wet bristle brush (see page 17).

DIRECTION OF LIGHT

LAY IN VALUES BEFORE MODELING THE HAIR

KEEP TWIGS BRITTLE

WATER

A.W.S. 300LB PAPER

EDGES HARD AT FIRST

SOFTEN EDGES WITH NO.3 BRISTLE BRUSH

3RD VALUE

1ST STEP LIGHT VALUE OVER ENTIRE FIGURE

2ND STEP 2ND VALUE

DO NOT SOFTEN EDGES UNTIL ALL VALUES ARE SET THEN USE THE NO 3 BRISTLE BRUSH

NO 7

YOUNG GIRL FROM MALAYA

Retaining the pure white of the paper for high lights is often essential in watercolor painting. As I've already mentioned, Maskoid can be very useful for this purpose. (See page 12.)

In the wash drawing opposite, I wanted to suggest a fluid, continuous motion in the movement of the water by using horizontal strokes cutting straight across the figure. However, I also wanted to retain the pure white of the paper for the high lights indicated. The drawings below show how Maskoid solved the problem.

1. APPLY MASKOID

2. PAINT BACKGROUND OF WATER HORIZONTALLY ACROSS FIGURE

3. REMOVE MASKOID AND DRAW FIGURE

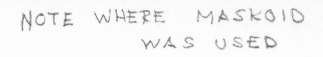

NOTE WHERE MASKOID
WAS USED
(ALL WHITE AREAS)

PAINTING A HEAD

As with painting the figure, painting the head requires a certain knowledge of the structure of the head, which can best be learned from books on anatomy and drawing. The step-by-step series opposite assumes you already know something about drawing the head. This is a simplified approach to painting it.

One color—sepia—was used for the demonstration, but any color could have been used, and of course the same emphasis on tonal values, working from light to dark, would be applicable to painting with a full-color palette (see pages 62, 76, 78, 80, 82, and 96, for example).

step 1. *Draw the head carefully, establishing source of light. In this demonstration the light is from overhead and a little to the right.*

step 2. *Erase pencil lines till they are hardly discernible. Apply light wash of sepia over entire head except for the whites of the eyes. While head is still wet, add darker note in cheek. Allow to dry.*

step 3. *Place darker values in all shadow areas such as neck, eye sockets and lips. Soften edges with bristle brush while modeling. Let dry.*

step 4. *Add darkest notes—hair, eyes and lips—and model each area as it is painted.*

50

1.

2.

3.

4.

PAINTING THE FIGURE IN COLOR

It isn't easy for a painter to catch the subtle variations in tone and color that give the appearance of warmth and life to flesh —but it has been a challenge to artists for centuries and undoubtedly will continue to be.

In the step-by-step discussions on pages 55, 60, 62, 75, 82 and 96, I have described the palettes and procedures for painting several different type models under varied lighting conditions. If you study these carefully, you will see that there is no single rule for painting flesh tones. For painting them in watercolor, though, it is wise to use a series of superimposed washes, always working from light to dark. The technique is the same as for the monochrome watercolors discussed on the previous pages, but now you work with different colors as well as tonal values.

NUDE — FOUR-COLOR PALETTE

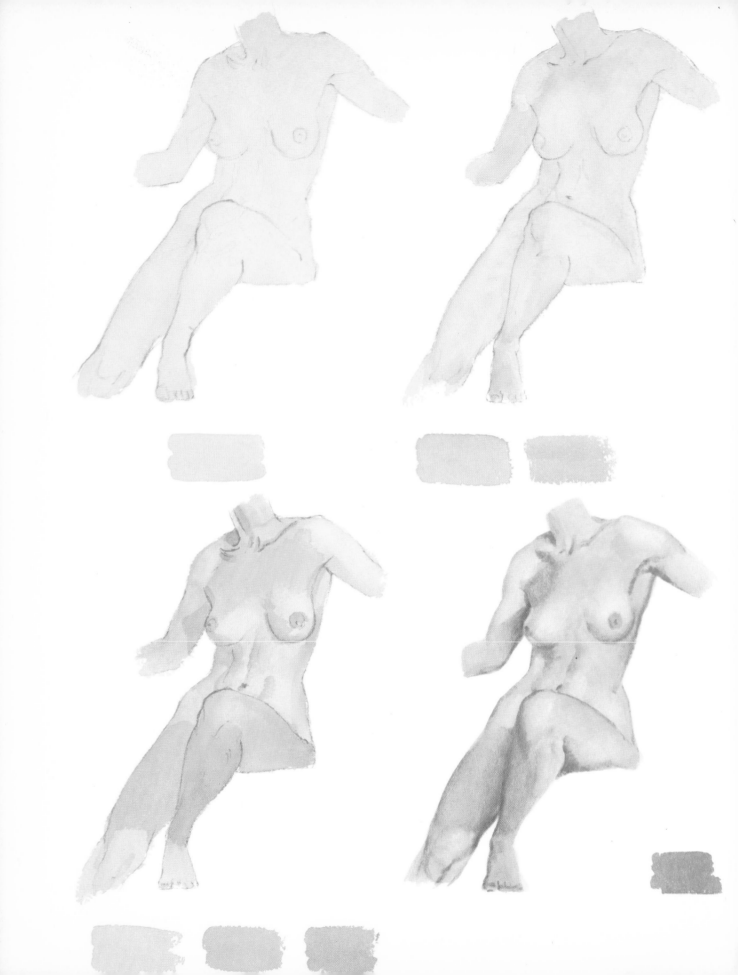

A FOUR-COLOR PALETTE

The color plate opposite shows what can be done with a simple four-color palette. The palette for this subject—a fair-skinned model—was limited to lemon yellow, burnt sienna, alizarin crimson and mauve.

The painting procedure is much the same as for the monochrome paintings on the preceding pages. Always work from light to dark, keeping tonal values as well as actual color values in mind. Here are the four steps in the development of this painting:

step 1. *Draw figure lightly, then wash with mixture of lemon yellow and burnt sienna.*

step 2. *While paper is wet, add alizarin crimson of same intensity shown in color swatch. Allow to dry.*

step 3. *Apply wash of burnt sienna and alizarin crimson, mixed on the palette, and allow to dry. This adds the shadow areas which give form to the body. In this painting the light source is from the right, so parts of both legs are in shadow.*

step 4. *Mix mauve with the other three colors and add to the shadow areas. Use bristle brush to blend color areas.*

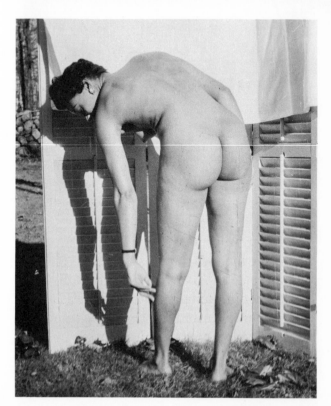

SELECTING THE MODEL

When painting from a model for the sole purpose of academic study, the actual subject is not particularly important. If you are planning a figure painting, however, the model should be chosen with care. A good professional model, the kind who is helpful and inventive, who knows how to take direction and can hold a pose, can be of great assistance to the artist. Whether you want a model who is old or young, lean or fat, short or tall, fair or dark, will depend of course on the concept of the picture in your mind.

Before you decide on the pose you want, it is often a good idea to let the model move around the studio for a while—twisting, turning, trying out poses that come naturally to her. If you can photograph her in some of these poses, you may have source material for many future studies and paintings.

If weather and environment permit, let the model work outdoors—as the model in these photographs did. The natural backgrounds and outdoor lighting suggested effects that would never have occurred to me in the studio.

MAKING THE SHADOW TELL THE STORY

Sometimes the shadow of a figure can be more important than the figure itself. In steps 1 and 2, below, where the figure is seen without a shadow, the effect is stilted and dull. The photograph and painting show a surprising shadow which gives new meaning to the pose. Who would have guessed she was brushing her hair?

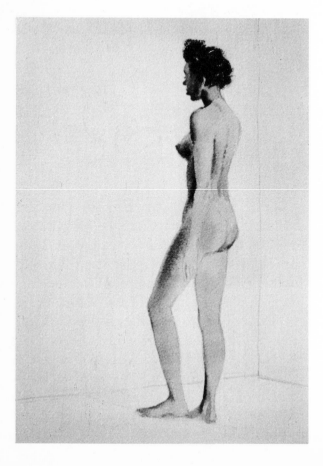

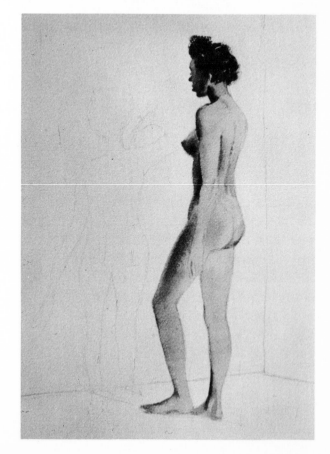

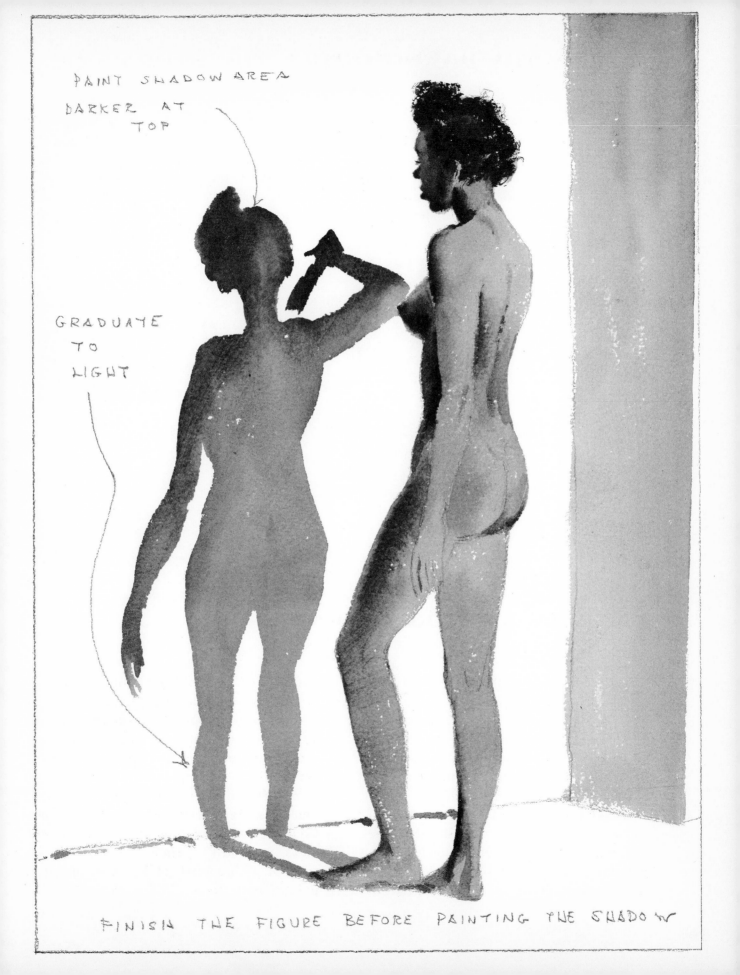

PAINT SHADOW AREA
DARKER AT TOP

GRADUATE
TO
LIGHT

FINISH THE FIGURE BEFORE PAINTING THE SHADOW

WHY NOT A BACK VIEW?

The back view of the figure is often ignored in painting the nude, yet the contour of the back has an easy-flowing grace and rhythmic line that is most beautiful. There are many examples of the back view of the nude in this book, including a step-by-step demonstration on page 46. The painting opposite shows the back view of a seated nude, a rather unusual pose. In "Locked Out," the color plate on page 63, there is still another back view—this time the standing figure of a very young girl.

PALETTE AND PROCEDURE

The flesh tones of the girl seated backwards are quite different from those of the nude on page 54. Although also fair-skinned, this model is seen in a strong artificial light which gives the skin a pale silvery look with just a touch of pink in the light areas, a green cast in the shadows. Yellow ochre, alizarin crimson, Hooker's green #2 and orange were used to paint the flesh tones.

The procedure for painting the figure was as follows: First, a light wash of yellow ochre went over the whole figure, hair included, and was allowed to dry. The legs, feet, arms and side of the back were then painted with Hooker's green and orange. When this was dry, the same colors were used again in the same areas, but with a little more green along the spine. Edges were softened with a bristle brush. A light tone of alizarin crimson was then washed over neck, buttocks and feet and into the areas previously painted. The hair was covered with a wash of burnt sienna, then painted with black.

LOCKED OUT

Here is a study in contrasts—animate against inanimate, warm against cool, young against old. These contrasts add a certain poignancy to the simple situation of a child locked out of the house after a swim.

step 1. Background and figure were drawn in carefully. Then the building—except for the door—was covered with a thin wash of black interspersed with tints of orange, cadmium red and burnt sienna. A thin wash of plain black was then put on the door. This gives the silvery wood on the side of the building a quality warmer than that of the door and also makes the figure appear warmer in contrast to the door. The window was painted with lemon yellow and black.

step 2. The figure was covered with a thin wash of yellow ochre. While this was still wet, burnt sienna and a light touch of alizarin crimson—mixed on the paper for a more vibrant effect—were added to the figure (except on the buttocks) and allowed to dry.

step 3. Mauve, burnt sienna and alizarin crimson, mixed on the palette, were added where darker flesh tones were needed.

step 4. Black, sepia, burnt sienna and permanent blue were used to paint the hair.

step 5. A very slight touch of blue was added where the buttocks blend into the top of the leg. Because of the under washes, this does not appear blue—it gives the effect of untanned skin. The only color on the light areas of the buttocks is the original wash of yellow ochre.

step 6. Texture was added to the building and door with several more washes of the same colors used in step 1. The wood was grained with darker tones of the same colors. The shadow of the figure on the door was done with the same colors as the door itself but intensified. The window shade was painted with lemon yellow and black mixed on the paper.

LOCKED OUT

FOLDS AND DRAPERIES

Fabrics of themselves are flat, two-dimensional and, in terms of form, without interest. But attach a piece of fabric to a support and it may turn into a beautiful bit of drapery; pull it taut across a three-dimensional object and its folds will describe the form beneath.

It is especially important for the figure painter to know how to handle folds and drapery. Whether painting a semidraped nude or a fully clothed figure, the problem is essentially the same: to show the form and the movement beneath the fabric by means of folds.

In painting folds, one thing must be kept in mind: Where there is a fold, there is a reason for it. When a fabric is pulled upward, you get one kind of fold; when allowed to fall, another. Every fold must have its support. The point of support and the pull determine the form the drapery takes. It either pulls or is being pulled; it clings or it falls; but the fabric does not become drapery until it is supported by something.

In the sketches on the next few pages I've shown some of the many things that can be said visually with folds. The number and quality of the folds will say something about the weight and texture of the fabric, for instance. The line of direction of the folds will indicate whether the fabric is stretched taut or hanging loose between two supports, whether it is falling free or lying in a limp mass on the floor. Folds can show a slight turn of the body or such vigorous actions as running or jumping—they can even show which way the wind is blowing.

As a rule, it is a good idea in painting folds to eliminate all unnecessary wrinkles, to simplify as much as possible. Exception: When painting a figure in a wet garment, use multiple folds to exaggerate the tight, clinging effect. Usually, though, too many folds on a draped figure will be disconcerting. Remember that folds are not only descriptive, they are also a decorative element in a picture and should be used with restraint.

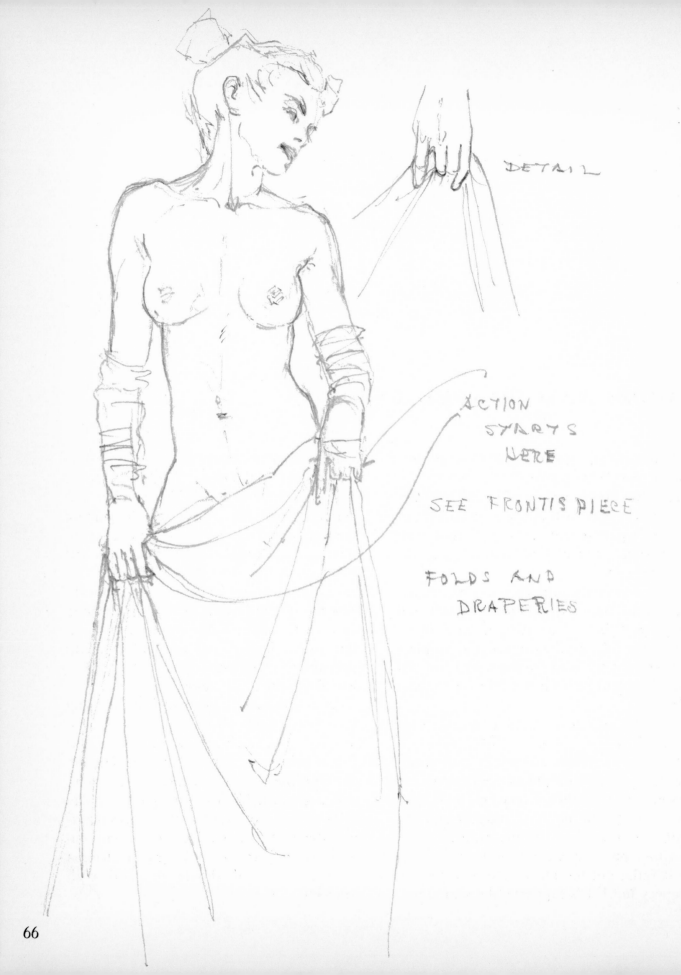

DETAIL

ACTION
STARTS
HERE

SEE FRONTISPIECE

FOLDS AND
DRAPERIES

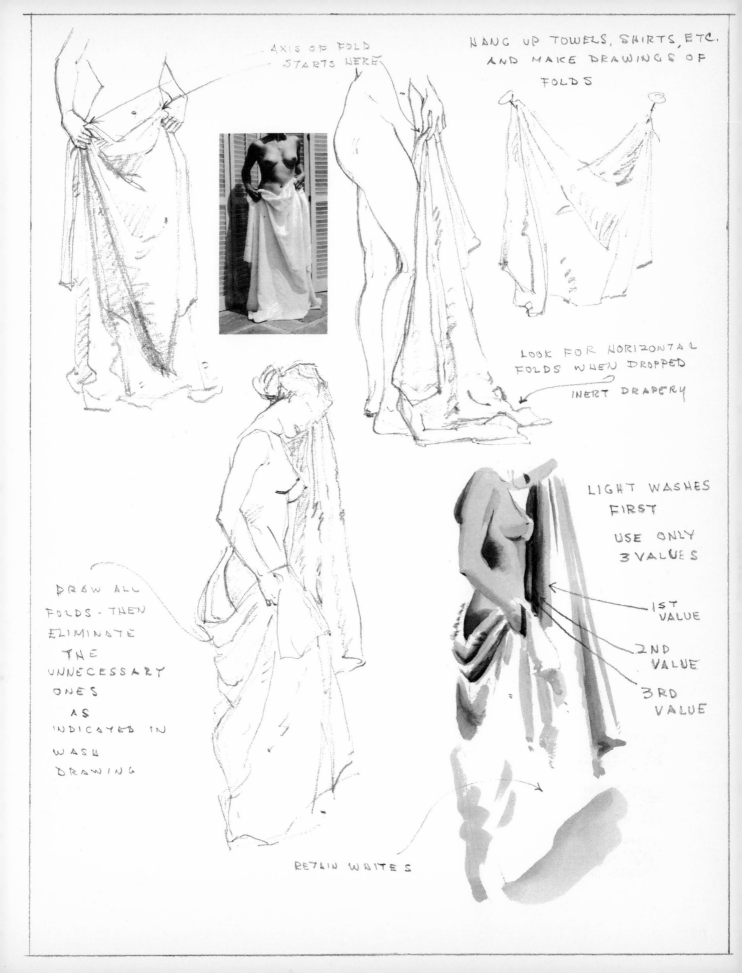

AXIS OF FOLD
STARTS HERE

HANG UP TOWELS, SHIRTS, ETC.
AND MAKE DRAWINGS OF
FOLDS

LOOK FOR HORIZONTAL
FOLDS WHEN DROPPED
INERT DRAPERY

DRAW ALL
FOLDS - THEN
ELIMINATE
THE
UNNECESSARY
ONES
AS
INDICATED IN
WASH
DRAWING

LIGHT WASHES
FIRST

USE ONLY
3 VALUES

1ST
VALUE

2ND
VALUE

3RD
VALUE

RETAIN WHITES

CAREFUL PL...
OF FOLDS WILL
RHYTHUM OF THE

FOLD S
FIGURE

...NING
...NHANCE THE
...GURE

AXIS OF FOLDS

CONVEX
...ONCAVE

FOLDS AND DRAPERIES

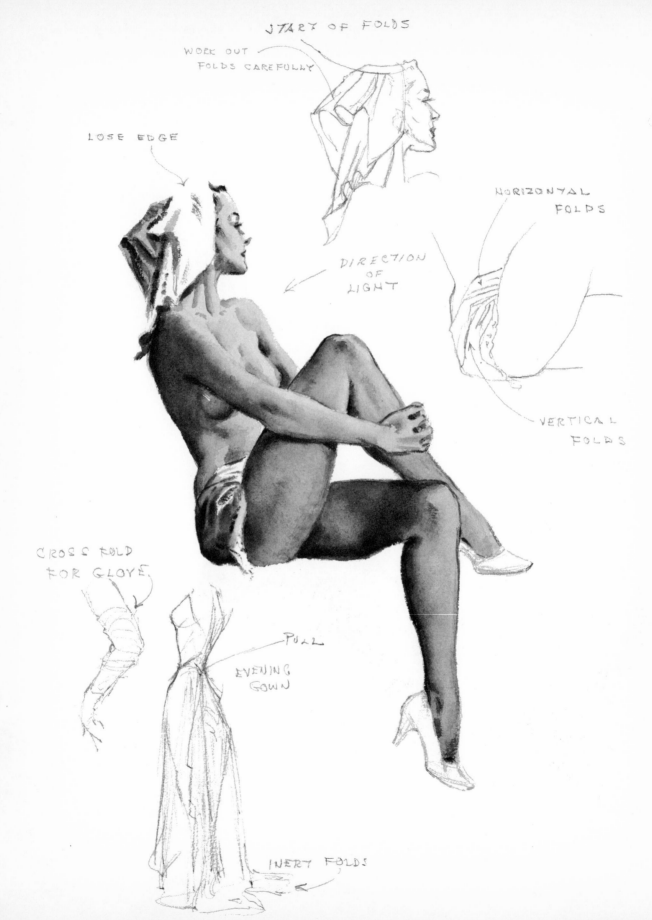

START OF FOLDS

WORK OUT
FOLDS CAREFULLY

LOSE EDGE

HORIZONTAL
FOLDS

DIRECTION
OF
LIGHT

VERTICAL
FOLDS

CROSS FOLD
FOR GLOVE

PULL

EVENING
GOWN

INERT FOLDS

70

PLEATED
FOLDS

FLOWING
ROBE

NOTE ACTION
OF FOLDS

RUNNING

SWIRLING
FOLDS

WIND

LIMP
FOLDS

71

SKIN TONES AND LIGHTING

What colors do you use to paint flesh tones? As I've mentioned before, it all depends. Factor one is the color of the model. Is she fair, ruddy or olive-skinned, Oriental or Negro? Obviously, different palettes will be required for different types of coloring.

Of equal importance is the kind of light the figure is viewed by. Early morning light is cool and so is the color of flesh seen in it. As the sun runs its course toward evening, the light becomes warmer and, in the late afternoon sun, flesh tones are likely to have a warm rosy glow. This can be seen, for example, in "Reflections in the Water," the color plate on page 19. A warm reflected light permeates this scene, so the figure was painted in hot colors: cadmium orange, lemon yellow, mauve and burnt sienna, with touches of orange added to the arms and legs after the figure was completed.

Flesh seen in artificial light will be affected by the color of the light itself and may appear to be almost any color.

So—there's no one formula for painting flesh. The figures in the color plate on page 74 show just four of many possible combinations of light source and skin tone. In the step-by-step demonstrations on pages 75-81 you will find the palettes and procedures for painting them.

LAST DAYS OF SUMMER   WASHLINE

SEPIA AND SURF   IN THE THICKET

SEPIA AND SURF

Some paintings demand a large palette, but for "Sepia and Surf" just three colors were used: burnt sienna, sepia and permanent blue. Here is how it was done:

step 1. *When the drawing was completed, a wash of burnt sienna was applied over the whole figure.*

step 2. *After the figure had dried, sepia was added for the darker areas and blended with the sienna. This was allowed to dry.*

step 3. *A light wash of permanent blue was applied to most of the figure, but not to the shoulders and head.*

step 4. *An eraser was used to pick out light areas on the shoulder blade, buttocks, legs, heels and arms.*

WASHLINE

step 1. a) *When the pencil drawing was completed, a yellow ochre wash—not too thin—was put over the entire figure.*
b) *While this wash was still wet, accents of burnt sienna were added where shadows were needed. Then the painting was allowed to dry.*

step 2. a) *The sky area was covered with a wash of yellow ochre. While this was wet, Antwerp blue, permanent blue and a touch of burnt sienna went over the yellow. This was allowed to dry.*
b) *The foreground was painted with Hooker's green and patches of burnt sienna mixed on the paper.*
c) *Permanent blue, cadmium orange, Payne's gray and burnt sienna, mixed on the paper, were used for the wall in the background. This was left to dry.*

step 3. a) *Getting back to the figure, a wash of sepia and burnt umber was added for the darker areas, taking care not to cover the first washes where light areas were to be retained.*
b) *Sepia, Indian red and cadmium red were mixed on the palette and used to add accent shadows.*
c) *After they had dried thoroughly, these dark areas or accent shadows were softened with a moist bristle brush.*
d) *A wash of alizarin crimson with a dash of cadmium red was floated over the entire figure. While it was wet, a slightly damp #12 sable brush was used to lift out certain areas in order to let the color of the previous wash show through. This helped to give form to the figure.*
e) *A thin wash of permanent blue was painted over the legs and buttocks.*

step 4. a) *The hair was painted with permanent blue, burnt sienna and black.*
b) *The stone wall was repainted, using the same colors as in step 2. While it was wet, the crevices between the stones were accented with black.*
c) *Hooker's green, black and lemon yellow, mixed on the palette, were used for the shadows in the foreground.*

step 5. a) *The figure was covered with a wash of Hooker's green and yellow ochre, then light areas were again picked out with a damp sable brush as in step 3. Repetition of this procedure makes the color appear vibrant.*
b) *There was a slight tendency for the figure to seem a bit too muscular or spotty, so it was covered with a final light wash of yellow ochre with a touch of cadmium red.*

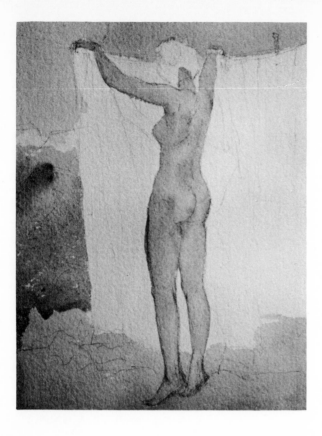 

LAST DAYS OF SUMMER

step 1. *When the light pencil drawing was completed, Maskoid was painted on the limbs of trees that were to remain white.*

step 2. *The sky was painted with yellow ochre, cobalt blue and a touch of Payne's gray. While this was damp, a crumpled rag was used to wipe off part of the color to create an effect of clouds (see page 15).*

step 3. *Horizontal strokes of permanent blue and a little umber were used to paint the sea. The heel of the brush created the shimmering effect.*

step 4. *A first wash of yellow ochre, cadmium orange and Hooker's green was applied to the figure and allowed to dry.*

step 5. *The Maskoid was removed and the limbs and branches of the trees were painted.*

step 6. *Cobalt blue, Antwerp blue, cadmium orange, cadmium red, alizarin crimson and burnt sienna were applied to the figure in thin washes mixed on the paper. This was done five times, allowing each wash to dry before applying the next. Edges were softened with a bristle brush after each wash.*

step 7. *Shadow areas were painted with deeper tones of the same colors.*

step 8. *Black, sienna, sepia and permanent blue were used for the hair.*

step 9. *The rocky ledge was painted with Payne's gray, cadmium orange, cadmium red and black.*

HORIZON

MASKOID

MASKOID ON
FIGURE IS
OPTIONAL

IN THE THICKET

step 1. *When the pencil drawing was completed, a wash of yellow ochre and orange with a tinge of Hooker's green was applied to the figure. This wash was extended about a half inch beyond the contour of the body to minimize hard edges around the figure.*

step 2. *When this was dry, the background was covered with lemon yellow to within a quarter inch of the figure.*

step 3. *With the background still wet, middle and darker notes were added with Hooker's green, sepia and Indian red, mixed on the paper. Twigs were added in the background and the painting was allowed to dry.*

step 4. *The figure was now painted with a series of washes of cobalt blue, mauve, burnt sienna, Hooker's green, cadmium orange, alizarin crimson and a tinge of cadmium red. Color accents were added while the paper was moist, not wet.*

step 5. *When the final wash was dry, cobalt blue was used to add the twigs in the foreground and the shadows of twigs on the figure.*

RIPPLES IN THE SAND

The beach is always a good background for outdoor figure painting. The form and color of sand and dunes provide a subtle compliment to the curves and skin tones of the human figure.

step 1. After the composition was established and the figure drawn, very lightly, in pencil, the sky was painted with permanent blue and yellow ochre.

step 2. An extremely thin wash of yellow ochre with tints of cadmium red and alizarin crimson was applied in all areas, including the figure, except the sky and allowed to dry.

step 3. A second thin wash of yellow ochre, cadmium orange, permanent blue and burnt sienna was applied to the same areas except for the figure and again allowed to dry.

step 4. Permanent blue, burnt sienna, cadmium yellow and a touch of burnt umber were mixed on the paper to paint the sand. Diagonal strokes starting from the top right cut across the picture but skipped the figure.

step 5. When the paper was dry, the shrubbery in the background was painted with the following colors, mixed on the paper:

sepia, burnt sienna, yellow ochre, Antwerp blue, Indian red and black.

step 6. Another thin wash was applied as in step 4. These two washes applied diagonally over the first wash helped create a feeling of depth in relation to the upper left portion of the picture, which was left light, and the lower part of the picture, which was intensified.

step 7. The figure was covered with a light wash of burnt sienna, lemon yellow and a touch of mauve where the skin tones are tanned; permanent blue, yellow ochre and burnt sienna for the untanned part. When dry, the values and edges of the two washes were softened with a damp bristle brush.

step 8. Burnt sienna, black and a touch of permanent blue were mixed on the paper for the hair. Cadmium red was used for the lips, mauve for the shadow area of the lips.

step 9. The accents in the sand in the lower right section were added with permanent blue, cadmium yellow orange, cadmium red and a touch of burnt sienna. When they were almost dry, the accent colors were blended into the background tones so that no pure colors are apparent in the finished painting.

PLANNING THE BACKGROUND

When planning a painting in which the figure will be shown in a rather detailed background, it is helpful to make preliminary drawings in which you experiment with various arrangements of elements in the picture before making a decision about the final composition.

The rather abstract composition opposite shows how one can use a drawing such as this to play around with perspective and horizon lines, setting the scale of the figure in relation to unidentified verticals, horizontals and curves.

The realistic drawing—which could be a further development of the abstraction—is the kind of detailed sketch with notes that helps the artist visualize the final painting. The details may actually be changed as he goes along, but this serves to remind him of what he is after.

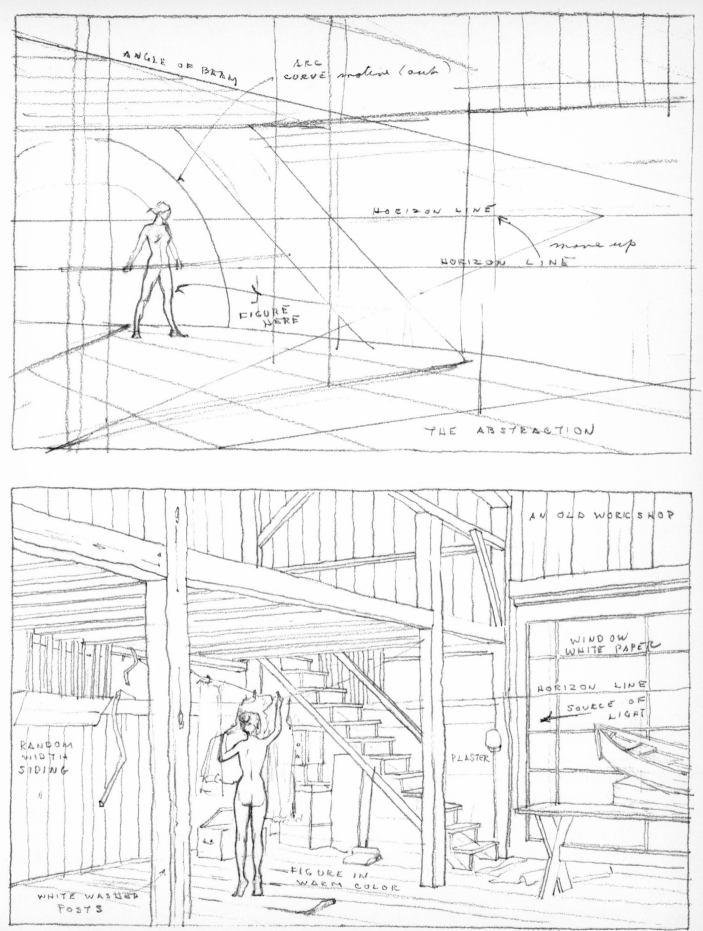

ANGLE OF BEAM ARC CURVE motive (out)

HORIZON LINE

HORIZON LINE   move up

FIGURE HERE

THE ABSTRACTION

AN OLD WORKSHOP

WINDOW WHITE PAPER

HORIZON LINE   SOURCE OF LIGHT

RANDOM WIDTH SIDING

PLASTER

FIGURE IN WARM COLOR

WHITE WASHED POSTS

BACKGROUND SUPPORT FOR THE FIGURE

The background of a figure painting should be interesting and well drawn, but it should always support the figure, never distract attention from it.

In the picture opposite, for instance, there is a strong vertical movement in the standing figure which is well supported by the structure, form and color of the draperies and the contrasting curves of the graceful Victorian chair.

The draperies were first painted in a sweeping vertical movement which was then counteracted by horizontal strokes as indicated. The color of the draperies could be a gray blue with the figure painted in warm tones—or this warm-cool complementary relationship could be reversed. Notice that the value next to the figure is a good deal darker than the rest of the drapery.

The chair, though carefully drawn, was painted freely—a good approach to all background painting.

The figure was also drawn in carefully but with as little detail as possible to avoid having pencil lines show through the painting.

HORIZONTAL PAINTING TO OFFSET VERTICAL BRUSHWORK

DIRECTION OF LIGHT

NOTE LACK OF DETAIL IN FIGURE

NOTE EDGES SOFT AND DARKER AROUND FIGURE

CHAIR AND DRAPES PAINTED FREELY

NOTE LONG SHADOWS

ADD CLOTHES HERE

SHADOWS DARKER AND THEN LIGHTER AS THEY LENGTHEN

WHICH FIRST — FIGURE OR BACKGROUND?

Although a simple background is often the best plan for a figure painting, a great amount of detail can be used without detracting from the importance of the figure —as "Girl with Newspaper" shows.

In one sense, however, this picture is an example of "how not to do it." The figure should never be painted first as it is here. Having completed the figure this far, it would be impossible—at least for me—to paint the background because no values have been established and the figure would have a "pasted in" look. Background and figure should always be worked together.

DOROTHEA

DOROTHEA

This painting shows how effective an out-door setting can be as a background for the figure. Here a very simple front view is dramatized by posing a Negro model against a whitewashed wall in strong sunlight, contrasting the dark skin tones against a bleached-out background. The sunlight creates pale high lights and deep shadow areas which model the form; it also throws an attractive shadow which repeats the curve of the figure on the wall. In the strong vertical lines and medium-to-dark tonal values of the doors there is good compositional support for the figure without distracting detail.

The step-by-step series on pages 96-97 shows how the painting was developed.

PROCEDURES FOR PAINTING DOROTHEA

step 1. After a careful drawing was completed, thin washes of Hooker's green, permanent blue, Rembrandt green, yellow ochre and burnt umber, mixed on the paper, were used to paint the doorway.

step 2. After the paper had dried, the figure—except for the hair—was covered with a thin wash of burnt sienna, which was then allowed to dry.

step 3. Dark accents were added to the shadow areas of the figure with sepia, burnt sienna and burnt umber; then edges were softened with a damp short-haired bristle brush.

step 4. While the figure was drying, more work was done on the door. Hooker's green was the base color, melded with yellow ochre, blues and burnt sienna to avoid a flat, posterlike effect. Darks were added with deeper tones of the same colors. The ground was painted with Payne's gray and burnt sienna. Notes of Hooker's green and yellow ochre were added to the grassy area while the paper was still wet. The textural effects on the wall were added by applying permanent blue, burnt umber and touches of orange with the flat side of the brush.

step 5. Getting back to the figure, all the deeper values were intensified and the various parts—arms, legs, torso—were modeled.

step 6. Accents were added to the figure using the same colors as in step 3—sepia, burnt sienna and burnt umber.

step 7. The hair was painted with a wash of permanent blue. Accents of black were added when the wash was dry and hard edges were softened.

step 8. Permanent blue, Indian red, cadmium orange and cadmium red, mixed on the paper, were used to paint the shadows and cracks on the wall.

CASEIN TECHNIQUES

Casein is a versatile medium, akin to both watercolor and oil in the ways it can be used and the effects it can produce. A finished casein painting may resemble a watercolor (though it will have less brilliance), or a gouache, tempera or oil painting—depending on the proportion of water used to dilute the pigments and on whether or not the surface of the painting is left with its natural mat finish. Mat-finish caseins are usually considered eligible for watercolor exhibitions; those that have been varnished or overpainted with oil glazes are disqualified in watercolor shows but are usually acceptable in exhibitions of oils.

One of the advantages casein has over oil is that it dries more quickly; one advantage over watercolor is that, once dry, a light color can be painted over a dark (white over red even) without the dark bleeding through. Of course, the quick drying can also be a disadvantage since casein dries light and chalky and is impervious to all solvents when dry. It is almost impossible to blend areas or match colors once the painting has thoroughly dried. Casein also has a tendency to crack after it is dry if too many or too-thick layers of color have been applied.

My approach to casein painting is quite different from my approach to watercolor. For one thing, I work from dark to light as I would in oil, rather than from light to dark as in watercolor. The reason for this is that in casein painting an opaque white is used—not only for pure whites but also to lighten other colors. (If they are lightened entirely with water, a more-or-less transparent watercolor effect will result.) Once casein white has been applied, it is extremely difficult to darken the areas it has covered. Incidentally, the white should be used sparingly or a chalky effect may result.

If casein is to be handled as a transparent medium, choose paper of the same quality as for a regular watercolor. For opaque casein paintings, however, rigid boards or panels may be used; it is not necessary to frame them under glass.

Extra precaution must be taken in the care of brushes when using casein; they should always be cleaned between painting sessions. A lanolin shampoo will keep them soft and pliable.

Detailed instructions distributed by the manufacturers of casein colors include many helpful suggestions for using casein as a transparent, opaque or mixed medium. Before starting to work in casein, it would be worth while to look over this material.

THE CASEIN PALETTE

The arrangement of my casein palette is very much the same as my watercolor palette with the colors arranged from warm to cool. However, the purple here is placed between cadmium red and alizarin crimson since it is closely related to the reds, whereas mauve (the purple in watercolor) leans more to the blues.

I use both Shiva and Grumbacher casein colors, but find the Shiva colors easier to work with because they dry more quickly. Of course, many artists prefer to have the pigment remain moist longer. This is entirely a matter of personal preference.

Here is my palette for Shiva casein colors:

warm colors

yellow ochre
cadmium yellow light
cadmium yellow medium
cadmium orange
cadmium red (extra scarlet)
selenium purple
alizarin crimson
burnt umber
burnt sienna

cool colors

ultramarine blue, deep
cobalt blue
Shiva blue, deep
Payne's gray
Shiva green
chrome oxide green, deep
terra verte
ivory black
titanium white

IN THE DRESSING ROOM

The figure here was blocked in first, the background last. Since the procedure for a casein painting such as this is the reverse of my watercolor technique, I painted the dark or shadow areas first, then the middle tones, finally the light ones. When the painting had dried sufficiently, I went over the entire surface, just as in watercolor painting, not concentrating on any one area but working them all together adding necessary detail and modifying tonal qualities.

For "In the Dressing Room" I used a limited palette: yellow ochre, chrome oxide, burnt sienna, terra verte, black, cadmium yellow light, burnt umber, cadmium red and white.

PLANNING A FIGURE COMPOSITION

"Stella," the casein painting reproduced in color on page 111, was not painted as a step-by-step demonstration for this book, so there is no analysis of the painting procedures that produced it. However, before it was painted, the pose, the composition and the lighting were carefully planned in a number of preliminary sketches which are shown on the following pages. The making of such sketches is the process that precedes step 1 of all my paintings—whether in watercolor, casein or oil.

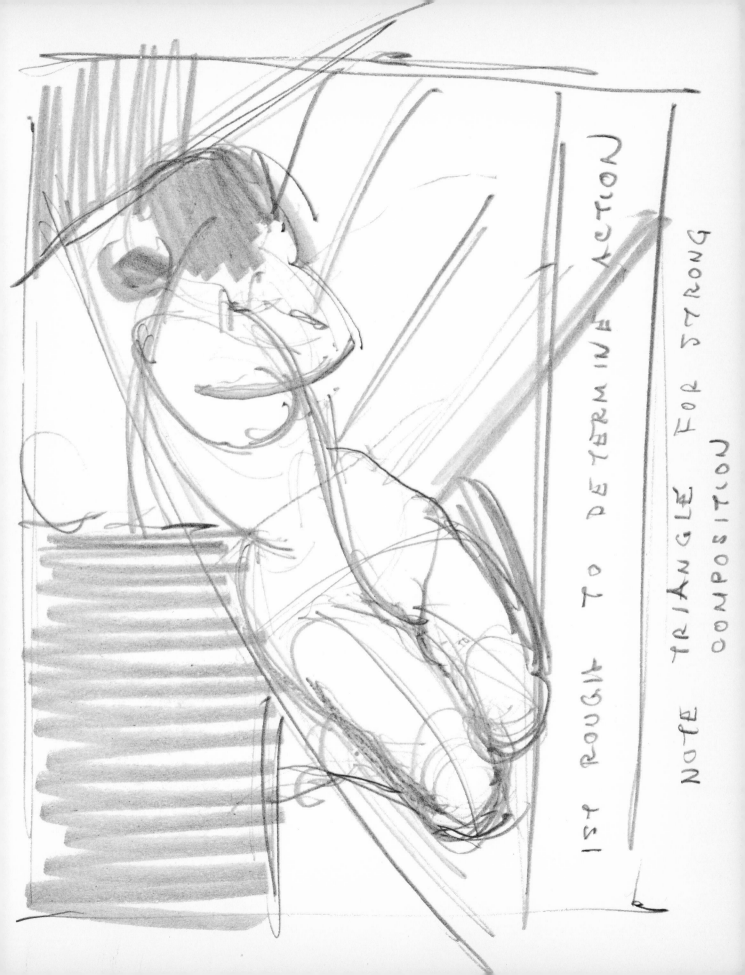

1st ROUGH TO DETERMINE ACTION

NOTE TRIANGLE FOR STRONG
COMPOSITION

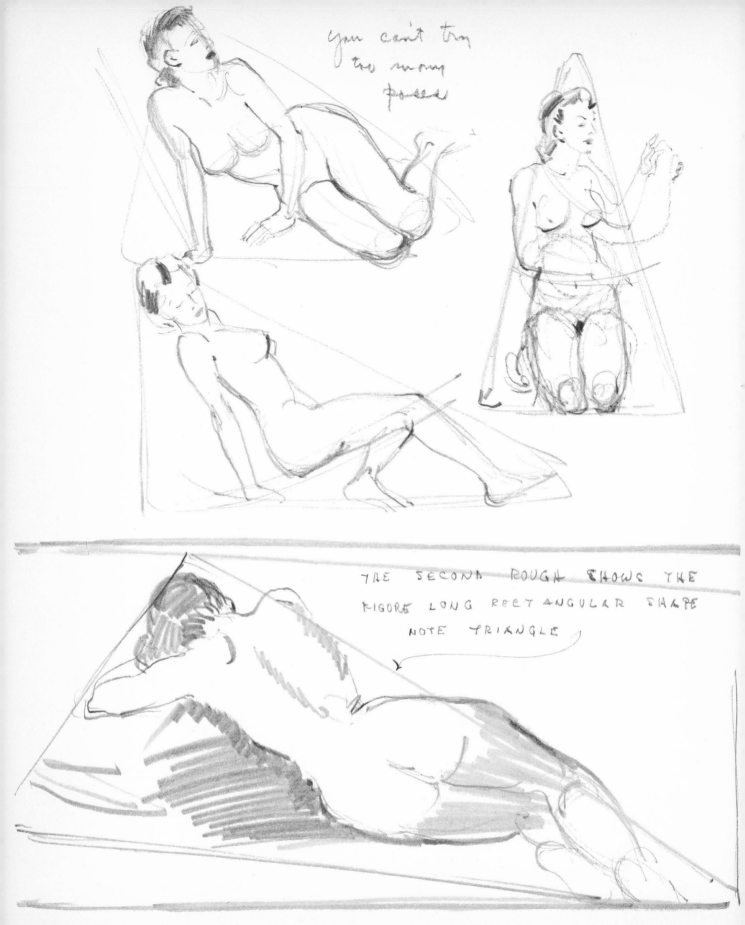

you can't try too many poses

THE SECOND ROUGH SHOWS THE
FIGURE LONG RECTANGULAR SHAPE
NOTE TRIANGLE

Try for
rhythm

easy flowing
lines

ON THE THIRD ROUGH I WENT
BACK TO NO1 EXCEPT THAT I
TRIED SHOWING THE HEAD

*Several rough wash drawings
helped to determine lighting in the painting.*

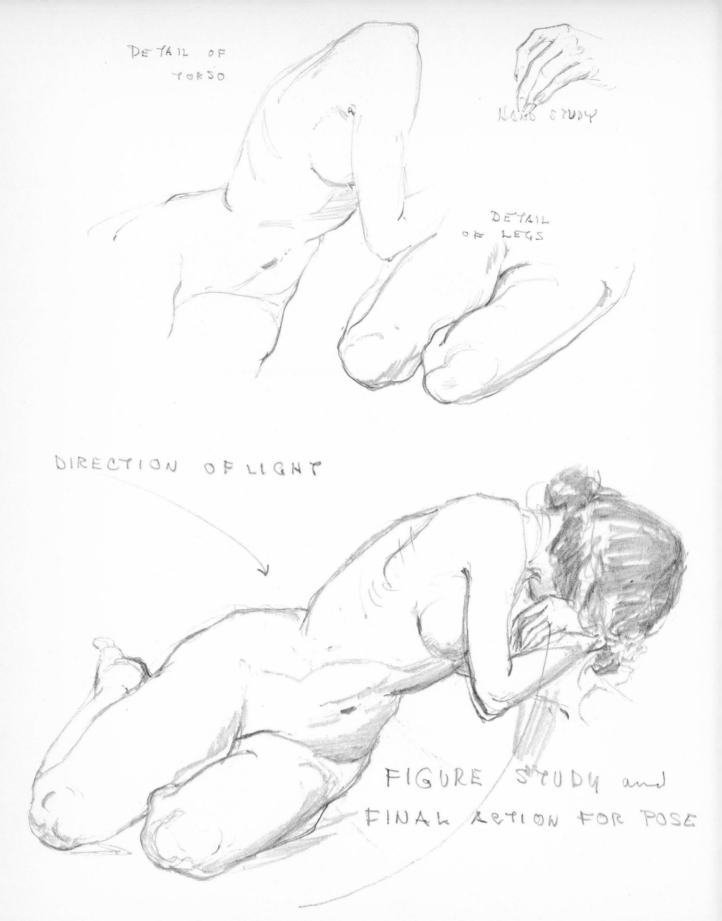

DETAIL OF
TORSO

HAND STUDY

DETAIL
OF LEGS

DIRECTION OF LIGHT

FIGURE STUDY and
FINAL ACTION FOR POSE

CHANGE HAND

DIRECTION OF LIGHT

FINAL STUDY FOR COMPOSITION RENDERED IN
WATER COLOR

SUBDUE WATER PITCHER

STELLA

"Stella" was painted with Shiva casein colors on rough Whatman Board. The original painting is 8 inches by 16 inches and was winner of the 1949 National Academy of Design Award.

The palette for the background was composed of burnt sienna, yellow ochre, selenium purple, chrome oxide, cobalt blue, Payne's gray, terra verte, black, cadmium yellow and white.

For the figure itself I used yellow ochre, cadmium yellow, burnt sienna, cadmium orange, alizarin crimson, chrome oxide, selenium purple, terra verte, cadmium red and white. The hair was painted with black, terra verte, cobalt blue and cadmium orange.

FROM THE COLLECTION OF
WILLIAM H. KUEHNEMAN, CHICAGO, ILLINOIS

STELLA

PUTTING SMALL FIGURES IN A SCENE

A figure can be important in a painting even when it is not the main subject. A small figure, for instance, can be used to establish the scale of other objects in the picture. More important, perhaps, is the animation a figure or group of figures can add to a painting that might otherwise seem dull and lifeless.

Throughout the book you will find examples of this use of small-scale figures in pictures that are essentially landscapes, street scenes or harbor scenes.

THE SIX-STEP FIGURE

When you want to add small-scale figures to a scene, it is not always necessary to do small detailed drawings. Often a much livelier effect can be achieved with the simple six-step figure, which gives an impression of form and action in a matter of seconds, all while wet.

This is how you do it.

step 1. *Paint head with one stroke of the brush.*

step 2. *Add neck and torso.*

step 3. *Add buttocks and breasts.*

step 4. *Add upper legs.*

step 5. *Add lower legs, feet and arms.*

step 6. *When the paper is dry, add lips, hair, shadow and any other accents.*

The procedure is essentially the same whether you're painting the front or back of a nude—as shown here—or clothed figures, such as the children in "Street Scene in Baltimore." Other examples of six-step figures can be seen in "Sailboats" (page 161) and "Harbor at Strawberry Bank" (pages 156-157).

WATERFALL

The scale of a small figure can compliment the grandeur of a large natural formation. In this picture I feel that the small figure is a perfect foil for the waterfall, emphasizing the dynamic force of the white water as it cascades down through the cold gray boulders.

In painting "Waterfall" I did not put the figure in until the rest of the picture was completed. Unlike the figures added to "Skier" (pages 128-135) and "Street Scene in Baltimore" (page 143), however, this one was planned from the beginning. In this case I simply found that, by waiting till the background was completed, it was easier to choose exactly the right spot to place the figure in relation to other elements of the composition.

QUARRY

The huge blocks of stone and granite in this composition provide excellent contrast for a figure—soft against hard, gentle curves against square and rectangular shapes. The background is not meant to be any specific place; it is simply an arrangement of shapes. I've called it "Quarry," but it might also suggest the ruins of an old Roman bath.

GROUPS OF FIGURES

A composition using a group of figures is an interesting challenge to a painter. Assuming you've started with a situation that required a group of people, there's the problem of how to handle them so that each figure will be effective in itself and also relate to the others in the group.

The figures in "Zoo" (pages 122-123) arranged themselves very conveniently for me one day when I was at the zoo with a Leica loaded with fast film. I took many quick candid snapshots of them and used several of the poses much as they were in the photographs (see above), changing others to improve the composition. I took considerable leeway with the color, trying to catch a certain carnival spirit which to me seems part of the whole atmosphere of a zoo. Much is left to the imagination of the viewer; no animals can be seen in the cages, yet you know they are there.

Incidentally, the halo effect around the figures was the result of one of those "happy accidents" watercolorists are always talking about. The irregularity of the surface of the paper caused this effect as I was painting the background. I hadn't planned it that way—but I liked it and kept it.

ZOO

PAINTING DIRECTLY FROM NATURE

Like many watercolor painters, I once believed that a watercolor should be painted on the spot—directly from nature, in one sitting—to have freshness and authenticity. I was wrong. The effectiveness of the final painting is not determined by where it is done or how long it takes to do it, but by the skill of the painter—how well he knows his business.

Furthermore, outdoor painting has many pitfalls. Most important is that light is constantly changing. If you start a picture in the late morning and finish it in the early afternoon, the light source will move from east to west while you are working. Unless you are very careful, your shadows and highlights may indicate more than one source of light—a mark of inexperience.

Tide is another problem. In a wharf scene such as "Harbor at Strawberry Bank" (pages 156-157), for instance, boats level with the dock when the picture is started may fall ten feet or more before it is finished. Often, too, a boat will pull out when you are only half through or another boat may pull in front of the one you've been painting and park there. The frustrations of outdoor painting are many.

My solution to these problems is to make quick color sketches, photographs and copious notes on the spot. (See "Watercolor Made Easy.") These provide me with source material on color, lighting and details which can be digested in the quiet serenity of my studio and used to create a painting. It is much more satisfying than simply copying a scene.

Of course, this procedure is only for the experienced painter. Beginners should first get experience painting outdoors under the guidance of competent instructors who are aware of its pitfalls. If you find that you enjoy painting directly from nature and prefer it to working indoors, you might try this approach: Instead of finishing a painting in one long session, plan to be at the scene at the same hour on several days—and then hope that the weather will be the same every day.

On the following pages are several types of outdoor scenes with suggestions on how to achieve some special effects.

BERMUDA STREET

A scene such as this would be empty without groups of figures to lend life and local color. The figures in the background were painted by the quick six-step method shown on pages 114-115; those in the foreground were drawn in carefully and painted in the usual way.

A WINTER LANDSCAPE

The painting demonstrated here was begun strictly as a winter landscape with snow —cold, lonely, with no sign of life. This is how it was painted:

step 1. a) *Using a sponge, I wet the areas in which I planned to paint the sky and the woods in the background.*

b) *A thin wash of yellow ochre was painted over this entire area while still wet. Cadmium red and yellow orange were added in the wooded area and continued into the sky while the paper was still wet.*

c) *I added permanent blue and Payne's gray to the top of the sky, using horizontal strokes running from one edge of the paper to the other. These colors blended.*

d) *While the paper was still wet, I painted the rear wooded area with Indian red, burnt umber, Hooker's green, sepia and Antwerp blue. Stroking vertically produced a soft look against the sky and a drybrush effect at the base of the wooded area.*

e) *Taking care not to cover the areas to remain white, I put a thin wash of permanent blue with a touch of Indian red over the large center area. The painting was now allowed to dry.*

step 2. a) *I added the shadow effects in the foreground, again using Indian red and permanent blue, but now more intense than in the previous step.*

b) *The buildings were painted with alizarin crimson, Indian red and lemon yellow.*

c) *Pine trees and brush were indicated with thin washes of Hooker's green, burnt umber and sepia for the firs, sepia and burnt umber for the brush.*

d) *Taking care not to let the colors run into the sky, I darkened the area at the base of the wooded section in the background by intensifying the colors used in step 1—Indian red, burnt umber, Hooker's green, sepia and Antwerp blue. The painting was again allowed to dry.*

step 3. a) *The snow in the area above the houses was intensified by painting from dark to light and keeping the edges toward the wooded section light. The snow area in the upper left of the picture was deepened.*
b) *Keeping in mind that the source of light was from the left, I put shadows on the houses.*
c) *Trees were added behind the buildings in the middle distance. Burnt umber, sienna and permanent blue were used for this.*
d) *I now intensified the firs and scrub: Hooker's green, umber and sepia again for the firs; burnt sienna, Indian red, burnt umber and permanent blue this time for the scrub. The painting was allowed to dry.*
e) *Trunks of large trees were put in, using sepia, black, Antwerp blue and burnt sienna.*
f) *To indicate tracks in the snow, I used deep tones of permanent blue and Indian red.*
g) *On the crest of the snow bank in the right foreground, I added a thin wash of yellow orange.*
h) *Before the painting was finished, I went over most of the areas again, intensifying them with the same colors used before. I added the wooded area back of the houses, the weeds and grass, telephone poles—but no wires. Vertical scratches with a knife gave the effect of birches and I scraped out a few high lights on twigs and stones. Finally, the hard edges were softened with a bristle brush.*

After the winter landscape was finished, I decided the composition would be improved if a figure were added. This is how I added it to the finished painting:

step 4. a) *Using a sponge and clean water, I deleted an area of road and shubbery to make room for the figure. (See photo above left.)*
b) *When the paper was dry, I drew the figure in very carefully. (See photo above right.)*
c) *The ski outfit was painted first in lemon yellow.*
d) *When this was dry, I added sepia and a light touch of blue for the shadow areas, then softened the effect with a bristle brush.*
e) *Burnt sienna, lemon yellow and a light touch of mauve were used to paint the face.*
f) *The shrubbery and snow areas around the figure were repainted as before and the shadow of the figure added.*

For the final effect, turn to the color plate on page 134

SKIER

SKIER

The finished painting complete with figure—now called "Skier"—demonstrates again how important even a small figure can be in a composition. Aside from its value in terms of composition, it also adds something to the mood of the painting. I had felt originally that without a figure the scene would suggest something of the lonely quiet of winter in the country. After the skier was added, however, I realized that the small figure—all alone and dwarfed by the snowdrifts—actually heightened this mood.

COLUMBUS CIRCLE

The misty effect of fog, rain or snow often lends beauty where none was seen before. In the painting opposite, the famous—but hardly beautiful—traffic circle in New York achieves a soft-focus glamour in the blur of fog, rain and dusk.

For hints on painting figures in foggy scenes, turn to page 138.

PAINTING FIGURES IN FOG

A point to remember when painting a misty scene is that the very haziness of the background heightens by contrast the apparent crispness of the foreground, especially objects that are the center of attention. In the pictures opposite showing the same foggy scene with and without a figure, you can see that the figure emerging from the mist is in sharp focus and that the background in this picture, by contrast, appears to be just a bit mistier. The figures in "Columbus Circle," on page 137, also appear much sharper than the background.

To paint a foggy scene, first erase your pencil drawing till it is just barely discernible, then sponge the entire surface of the paper with clean water until it is very wet.

While the paper is quite damp, paint the background with thin washes of light, cool colors. Gradually work from background to foreground, increasing the intensity of the colors as you work forward. The closer the object, the sharper the focus and the more accurate the colors.

The sharpness of touches of pure white can be very effective in foggy scenes—as the white hatband in the demonstration opposite shows. It was saved by Maskoid, of course, as were the pure white areas in "Columbus Circle." The effect of diffused light around the lamppost in that picture was achieved with a sand eraser, using a circular movement; nicks with a knife produced the effect of rain.

FIGURES IN A FALL SCENE

The transparent brilliance of fall foliage is always a temptation and a challenge to the painter and especially to the watercolorist. The addition of small figures to a country scene such as this gives a sense of scale and also permits the use of sharp notes of pure color in the clothes to contrast with the subtle variations of tone in the foliage.

step 1. *After a careful drawing was made, the sky was painted with a light wash of permanent blue mixed with just a touch of burnt umber.*

step 2. *A mixture of permanent blue and sepia, the blue predominant, was used for the hills.*

step 3. *A wash of lemon yellow was applied as a base for the foliage, trees and grass.*

step 4. *The darker notes of the trees in the background were added with cadmium yellow, cadmium orange and cadmium red, interspersed with Hooker's green.*

step 5. *Payne's gray, black and orange were used for the stone wall, the colors being blended together with a damp bristle brush. Accents on the stones were added with black and alizarin crimson, mixed on the paper.*

step 6. *Light washes of cadmium orange, cadmium red and touches of Hooker's green were added to the foliage in the foreground. When this was dry, twigs were added.*

step 7. *Sepia, burnt sienna and permanent blue—not too dark—were used to paint the tree trunks in the background. Those in the foreground were painted black—with Rembrandt green added at the base, sepia in the middle, then burnt sienna vibrating back to black toward the top.*

step 8. *Cadmium red, with black added for the shadow area, was used to paint the houses at the left.*

step 9. *Permanent blue and orange, mixed on the paper, were used for the shadow areas on the white houses.*

step 10. *The shadow of the tree on the road was painted with Payne's gray and a touch of orange.*

step 11. *For the grasses along the road, burnt sienna and Hooker's green, accented with sepia, were painted over the original lemon yellow wash, letting patches of the yellow show through.*

step 12. *The light area of the road was covered with a thin black wash before the shadows in the foreground were added. Payne's gray, darker at the base, was used for the shadows of the figures.*

step 13. *The figure of the boy was painted with cadmium red for the pants, permanent blue for the sweater. The girl's white dress is mostly the white of the paper. The skin tones of both figures are deep tan.*

step 14. *The shadows of the figures were painted with Payne's gray—darker at the base of the figures.*

STREET SCENE IN BALTIMORE

Painted as an impression of the old section of Baltimore rather than of one particular street, this picture was based on a great many photographs of details of the area—narrow streets, cobblestones, old stairways. When I had finished painting it, however, I was dissatisfied with the result (see photo above). Something was missing.

Eventually, I realized it needed figures to add a bit of life to it. The old woman was drawn in carefully and painted in the usual way. The children were added by the quick six-step method of figure painting described on pages 114-115.

If you study the detail opposite, you can see how it was done.

STREET SCENE IN BALTIMORE

FULL SIZE DETAIL

EXPERIMENT WITH COLOR

EXPERIMENTS WITH COLOR

Once an artist has become familiar with his tools and materials and has developed his own way of working, there is often a tendency to rely on particular effects produced in what may have become dependable, "fool-proof" ways. This is where formula painting sets in.

To avoid succumbing to this temptation, it is necessary to experiment constantly with new ways of handling familiar problems. With this in mind I set out to find new combinations for producing flesh tones.

I began by covering a large sheet of paper with daubs of every color on my palette, letting them bleed into each other—green into blue, blue into orange, Payne's gray into burnt sienna. I then drew a figure on tracing paper and, when the motley background was dry, moved the figure over the colors until I found an area that particularly pleased me. The figure was then traced onto the background and outlined with Rich Art White to distinguish the color of the figure from the background colors.

You can easily experiment this way yourself. Use the cut-out that accompanies this book over your own sheets of daubed color —or make your own cut-outs if you prefer.

ABOUT ABSTRACTION

A lot of sound and fury has raged about abstract art since Marcel Duchamp's nude descended a staircase in the famed Armory Show of 1913, and it is not my intention to add fuel to the old argument now. I do not decry abstract art. If a painter is honestly seeking a way of expressing an idea or emotion which he feels cannot be stated in conventional terms, there is no reason why he should be limited to traditional pictorial expression.

My own creative processes require realistic expression and my use of abstraction—which is the isolation of "pure" form from recognizable objects—is limited almost entirely to the division of space. However, it can be very stimulating for a representational painter to start thinking in terms of solid masses and fundamental forms. The imagination is prodded by the exercise, and interesting effects often evolve as the objects and spaces between are broken down into basic shapes. In fact, as the experiments on the following pages suggest, playing with abstraction—like playing with color—can be fun.

The painting opposite is a kaleidoscope of abstract color forms. To me, it suggests the razzle-dazzle of a summer day at the beach so I've called it "Seaside Resort."

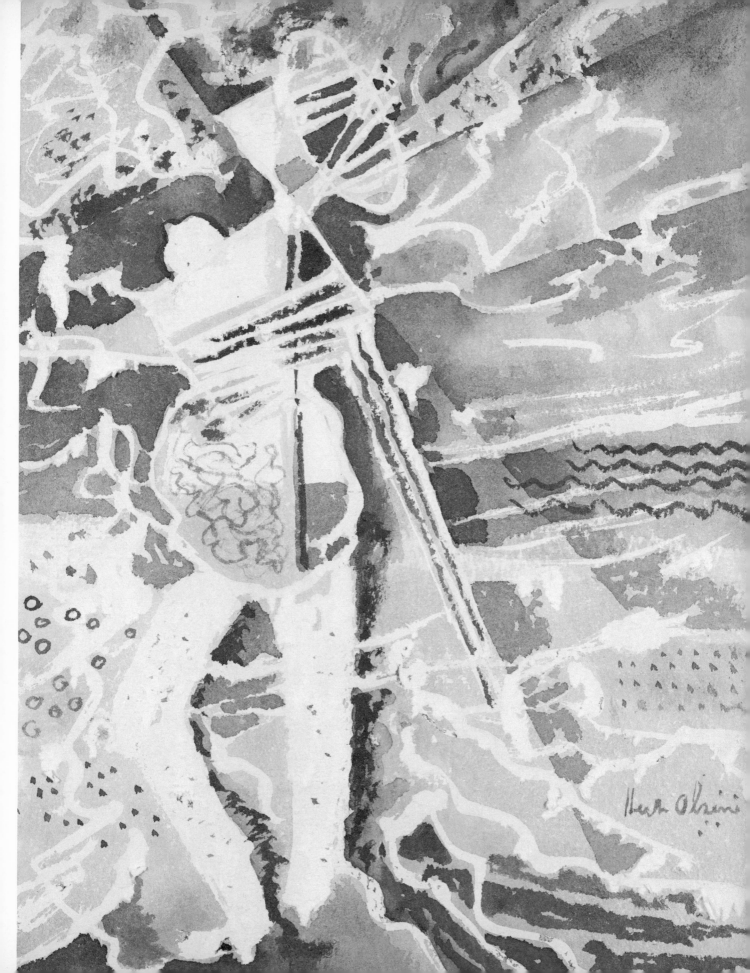

Here the female figure has been reduced to abstract elements of cubes, triangles and rectangles as a step toward its reconstruction as pure geometric form.

SQUARE

TRIANGLE

MAKE SEVERAL FORMS BEFORE DOING YOUR FINAL ABSTRACTION

USE MODEL FOR MOTION OR ACTION

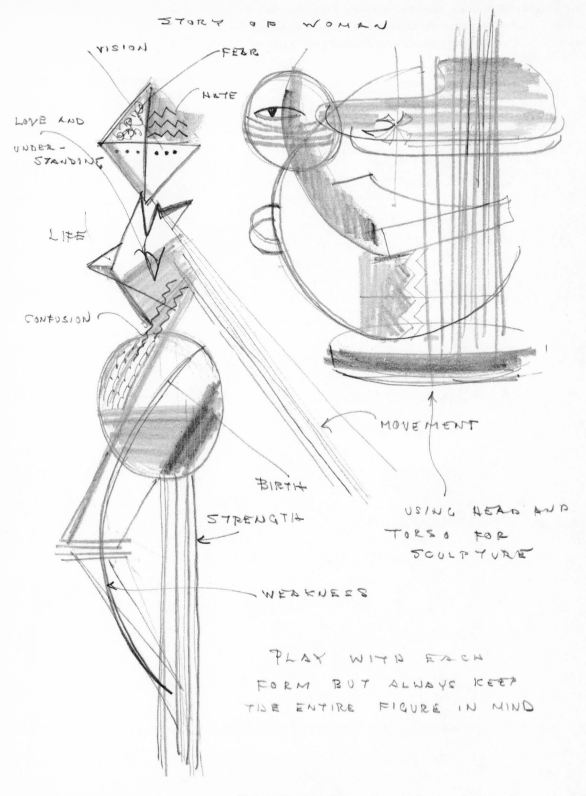

This whimsical abstraction of the female form is a rhythmic design based on circular and linear movements.

These rough sketches show how recognizable form can be broken down into abstract components. Sketch #1 is still semirealistic. The other three are variations on the female figure in terms of squares, circles and triangles.

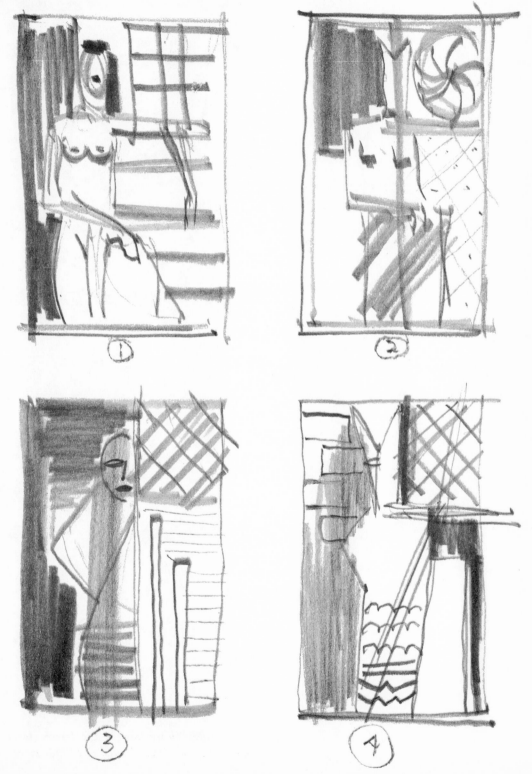

The abstract components of the sketches above are here rearranged in another interpretation. Though far from realistic, the figure is still recognizable as such.

Hunt Olsen

153

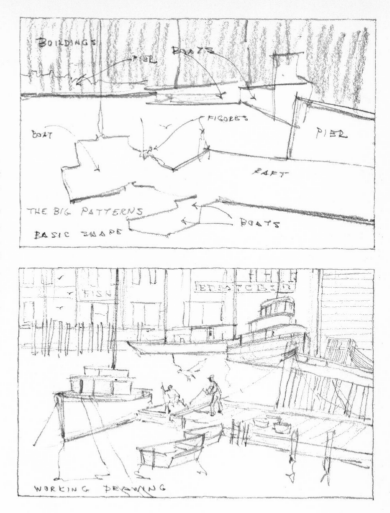

In planning the composition of "Harbor at Strawberry Bank" (pages 156-157), I made the preliminary pencil sketches shown above. The first was simply an arrangement of the main elements of the picture in terms of abstract shapes. The second, the realistic interpretation of these shapes, was the final basis for the painting itself.

HARBOR AT STRAWBERRY BANK

This painting is still another example of the importance of small-scale figures in a large composition. The men on the pier, though painted quickly in the six-step manner, are the center of attention. Much is said about them and the work they are doing with just a few brush strokes. Even at this size, knowledge of anatomy and the way the body moves is essential.

The reflections in the water are also important in this picture. Here's how they were done:

The buildings and all the objects that would be reflected were painted first, then, before the water was painted, the reflections were painted in the same colors as the objects which they reflect. When this was dry, Maskoid was applied to all areas that were to remain white. This made it easier to achieve a feeling of fluid movement in the water which could then be painted freely without worrying about accidentally running a wash into a white area.

When the Maskoid was dry, the water was painted right over the reflections—using a two-inch brush and horizontal strokes

HARBOR AT STRAWBERRY BANK

for the large areas, an Aquarelle for the swirling movements. A wash of permanent blue was applied first, followed by a wash of Hooker's green with a touch of sepia, the two washes blended wet on the paper, the blue predominant. The dark foreground was painted with Payne's gray, sepia, yellow ochre and Hooker's green, blended on the paper. While this was damp, alizarin crimson and sepia were added to the reflection of the larger boat. The reflection of the small white boat and the light reflection of sky in the foreground were wiped out with a damp rag and a sponge. At this point, the water appeared thin, so two additional washes of the colors originally used were applied. The light areas were wiped out and the paper allowed to dry thoroughly after each wash. When the color values were right, the Maskoid was removed and edges were softened with a damp bristle brush.

If you study the color reproduction, you can see how the original color of the underpainted reflections comes up through the superimposed washes and adds depth to the painting.

MINUTE FIGURES CAN BE IMPORTANT

Even a minute figure, seen at a distance, can be important if the figure is appropriate to the subject and placed properly in the composition.

The tiny figures in "Sailboats" were painted by the six-step method. Although they appear as indistinct silhouettes in this black-and-white reproduction, the small touches of cadmium red in the caps and jackets are important accents in the original color painting.

The procedures for painting this picture involved several helpful hints that are useful in painting sea- and sky-scapes. Before starting to paint at all, the area below the horizon line was completely covered with Scotch tape to prevent the sky washes from running into the sea. I particularly wanted to keep a line of white where sea meets sky at the horizon.

To paint the sky, I first sponged on a heavy wash of water, then applied a very light wash of yellow ochre and cadmium red to the lower half of the sky, permanent blue and Payne's gray to the upper half, and added umber in the darker middle area. The white areas in the sky were wiped out with a rag and then, while the paper was still very wet, I added dabs of sepia and burnt umber for clouds and immediately tilted the paper from side to side and up and down to make the colors run, giving the clouds a soft feathery look. As soon as I had the effect I wanted, the paper was placed on a level table to dry. If this had not been done, the sky would have run off and the effect would have been lost.

When the paper was dry, I removed the Scotch tape and painted the water. For the shimmering effect, I applied a dry, light wash of Rembrandt green and permanent blue with the heel of the Aquarelle brush. The sea in the foreground was painted with Payne's gray, permanent blue and umber. While this was still wet, criss-cross strokes of deeper values of the same colors added the wavy effect. Care was taken to keep the paper flat on the level table.

The silhouettes of the boats were painted with very dark tones of sepia, alizarin crimson and Antwerp blue. The small figures and reflections were added last.

PUTTING A FIGURE IN A "SLOT"

One good way to dramatize a figure is to put it in a "slot." In "Tyson Street," opposite, this is done by showing the figure in a narrow street between buildings which, by comparison, seem tall. A "slot" is a device of composition. It may encompass only a small part of the total area of the painting, but by serving as a focal point it becomes the most important part of the picture.

"Tyson Street," by the way, is an old street in Baltimore recently restored by a group interested in preserving the old houses, gas lamps and nostalgic atmosphere of another day.

CITY STREET

This is another example of "slot" composition. Here the buildings on the left occupy three-quarters of the picture, yet one's eye goes immediately to the figures in the small open space on the right.

"City Street" was awarded the Adolph and Clara Obrig Prize at the 128th Annual Exhibition of the National Academy of Design and was purchased by the National Academy for the Henry Ranger Fund.

165

Knowledge is but the academic test
Of ignorance; a question of degree;
And he who knows the most, knows best of all
How much there is he cannot know.

FROM "BEGINNINGS"

BY JAMES BATTERSON